EUROPEAN UNION AND TRADE BARRIERS IN EUROPE

EUROPEAN UNION AND TRADE BARRIERS IN EUROPE

PAULA R. LIGNELLI

Nova Science Publishers, Inc.
New York

For permission to use material from this book please contact us:
Telephone 631-231-7269; Fax 631-231-8175
Web Site: http://www.novapublishers.com

LIBRARY OF CONGRESS CATALOGING-IN-PUBLICATION DATA

European Union and trade barriers in Europe / Paula R. Lignelli (editor).
p. cm. ISBN 978-1-60456-742-7 (softcover)
1. Europe--Commercial policy. 2. European Union countries--Foreign economic relations. 3. Foreign trade regulation--European Union countries. 4. Non-tariff trade barriers--European Union countries . 5. Tariff--European Union countries. I. Lignelli, Paula R. HF2033.E872 2008
382'.3094--dc22 2008018260

Published by Nova Science Publishers, Inc. ✣ New York

CONTENTS

PREFACE

The U.S. goods trade deficit with the European Union was $116.6 billion in 2006, a decrease of $5.7 billion from $122.3 billion in 2005. U.S. goods exports in 2006 were $214.0 billion, up 14.8 percent from the previous year. Corresponding U.S. imports from the European Union were $330.6 billion, up 7.1 percent. European Union countries, together, ranked second behind Canada as an export market for the United States in 2006. U.S. exports of private commercial services (i.e., excluding military and government) to the European Union were $127.8 billion in 2005 (latest data available), and U.S. imports were $105.9 million. Sales of services in the European Union by majority U.S.-owned affiliates were $249.1 billion in 2004 (latest data available), while sales of services in the United States by majority European Union-owned firms were $224.3 billion. The stock of U.S. foreign direct investment (FDI) in the European Union in 2005 was $949.0 billion (latest data available), down from $973.0 billion in 2004. U.S. FDI in the European Union is concentrated largely in the non-bank holding companies, manufacturing, finance, and wholesale trade sectors.

Chapter 1

Overview

In most respects, the enormous United States-EU trade and investment relationship operates smoothly and to the great benefit of companies, workers, and consumers on both sides of the Atlantic. In recognition of this fact, leaders of the United States and the European Union agreed, in the context of the June 2005 United States-EU Summit (reaffirmed at the June 2006 United States-EU Summit), to pursue additional transatlantic economic integration through a series of cooperative initiatives in areas such as regulatory cooperation, intellectual property rights enforcement, innovation, and trade and security, among other issues.

Despite the broadly positive nature of the United States-EU trade and investment relationship, U.S. exporters in some sectors continue to face chronic barriers to entering the EU market. A number of these barriers have been highlighted in this report for many years, despite repeated efforts to resolve them through bilateral consultations or, in some cases, the dispute settlement provisions of the WTO.

Over the course of the past year, U.S. concerns continued regarding the EU's longstanding policy of subsidizing the development, production, and marketing of large civil aircraft. In general, barriers to access for U.S. agricultural exports continue to be a source of frustration for the United States. Even where formal EU agricultural tariff barriers may be relatively low, U.S. exports of leading commodities such as corn, beef, poultry, soy, pork and rice are significantly restricted or excluded altogether due to restrictive EU non-tariff barriers or regulatory approaches that often do not reflect a sound assessment of actual risks posed by the goods in question. In addition, the trade-distorting effects of various EU Member State policies governing pharmaceuticals and health care products are generating concerns related both to market access and to healthcare innovation. This year's report also outlines concerns of U.S. exporters with respect to a number of emerging EU policies that may threaten to disrupt trade in the future, such as the proposed new EU chemicals regulation.

On October 17, 2006, the EU Council approved Romania and Bulgaria's accession to the European Union, and the two countries joined the EU on January 1, 2007. Because Romania and Bulgaria began adopting EU laws and regulations in the lead-up to their accession to the EU, this report includes a discussion of enlargement-related trade policy issues as well as other barriers in the Romanian and Bulgarian markets.

Chapter 2

IMPORT POLICIES

CUSTOMS ADMINISTRATION

Notwithstanding the existence of a body of EU customs law, the EU does not operate as a single customs administration. Rather, there is a separate agency responsible for the administration of EU customs law in each of the EU's 27 Member States. The 27 separate agencies do not administer EU customs law in a uniform manner, as is required by Article X:3(a) of the General Agreement on Tariffs and Trade 1994 ("GATT 1994"). No EU institutions or procedures ensure that EU rules on classification, valuation, origin, and customs procedures are applied in a way that remains the same from Member State to Member State. Moreover, no EU rules require the customs agency in one Member State to follow the decisions of the customs agency in another Member State with respect to materially identical issues.

On some questions, where the customs agencies in different Member States administer EU law differently, the matter may be referred to the Customs Code Committee. The Committee is an entity established by the Community Customs Code to assist the European Commission. The Committee consists of representatives of the Member States and is chaired by a representative of the Commission. While, in theory, the Committee exists to help reconcile differences among Member State practices and thereby help to achieve uniformity of administration, in practice its success in this regard has been limited.

Not only are the Committee and other EU-level institutions ineffective tools for achieving the uniform administration of EU customs law, but the EU also lacks tribunals or procedures for the prompt review and EU-wide correction of administrative actions relating to customs matters. Instead, review is provided separately by each Member State's tribunals – and rules regarding these reviews can vary from Member State to Member State. Thus, a trader encountering non-uniform administration of EU customs law in multiple Member States must bring a separate appeal in each Member State whose agency rendered an adverse decision. Ultimately, a question of interpretation of EU law may be referred to the Court of Justice of the European Union (ECJ). The judgments of the ECJ have effect throughout the EU. However, referral of questions to the ECJ generally is discretionary and ECJ proceedings can take years. Thus, obtaining corrections with EU-wide effect for administrative actions relating to customs matters is a cumbersome and frequently time-consuming process.

The United States has raised both of the foregoing sets of concerns with the EU in various fora. The concerns have taken on new prominence in light of the expansion of the EU (which now includes 27 Member States) and the focus of the Doha Development Agenda on trade facilitation. Given the growing negative consequences of deficiencies in the EU's customs administration and review procedures, the United States initiated WTO consultations in September 2004. Subsequently, in March 2005, a dispute settlement panel was formed to consider U.S. complaints.

On June 16, 2006, the panel circulated its report, in which it found a lack of uniform administration in certain specified instances, and found no breach of the EU's obligations with respect to prompt review and correction of customs determinations. The United States and EU each appealed different aspects of the panel report. In its report issued on November 13, 2006, the Appellate Body agreed that the panel had misread the U.S. complaint. The Appellate Body also agreed with the United States on certain other legal points and agreed with the EU that the panel had erred in finding non-uniform administration in two particular instances. Finally, the Appellate Body agreed with the panel's finding of no breach of the EU's obligation regarding prompt review and correction of customs administrative action.

The panel and Appellate Body reports were adopted at the December 11, 2006 meeting of the WTO Dispute Settlement Body. The reports as adopted included a finding that the EU is in breach of its obligation of uniform administration with respect to rules pertaining to the tariff classification of certain liquid crystal display monitors.

EU ENLARGEMENT

In anticipation of the accession of Romania and Bulgaria to the EU on January 1, 2007, the United States in December 2006 entered into negotiations with the EU within the framework of GATT provisions relating to the expansion of customs unions. Upon their accessions, Romania and Bulgaria were required to change their tariff schedules to conform to the EU's common external tariff schedule, resulting in increased tariffs on certain products imported into Romania and Bulgaria from third countries. Under General Agreement on Tariffs and Trade 1994 (GATT 1994) Articles XXIV: 6 and XXVIII, the United States is entitled to compensation from the EU to offset some of these changes. The expansion of pre-existing EU quotas to account for the addition of Romania and Bulgaria to the European Union common market is another key element of the negotiations. This round of enlargement presents particular issues for exporters to Romania and Bulgaria of key commodities such as pork, which will face a significant increase in applied tariff rates and the imposition of quotas. In 2007, the United States will seek to conclude an appropriate bilateral compensation agreement with the European Commission and ensure that its benefits are implemented as soon as possible.

On March 22, 2006, the United States and the EU signed a bilateral agreement within the framework of the GATT related to the May 2004 enlargement of the European Union. As part of the agreement, the EU opened new country-specific tariff-rate quotas for U.S. exports of boneless ham, poultry, and corn gluten meal. It expanded existing global tariff-rate Quotas for food preparations, fructose, pork, rice, barley, wheat, maize, preserved fruits, fruit juices, pasta, chocolate, pet food, beef, poultry, live bovine animals and sheep, and various cheeses and vegetables. It permanently reduced tariffs on protein concentrates, fish (hake, Alaska Pollack, surimi), chemicals (polyvinyl butyral), aluminum tube, and molybdenuym wire. These unilateral EU concessions went into effect in July 2006.

In addition to tariff changes, the adoption of EU non-tariff barriers by acceding member states has resulted in the loss of significant markets for U.S. exports of poultry, and severely restricted U.S. exports of other agricultural commodities (see Sanitary and Phytosanitary section).

In 2003, to address potential incompatibilities between Bilateral Investment Treaty (BIT) obligations and EU law, the United States and Romania and Bulgaria agreed to make several narrow amendments to the texts of their respective BITs. Both the United States and these two countries have ratified the BIT amendments, and the amendments entered into force upon an exchange of instruments. This exchange took place in Bulgaria on January 16, 2007, and in Romania on February 9.

The customs administration issues noted above for the EU will only become more complex with the addition of Romania and Bulgaria. In Bulgaria, in particular, exporters have reported inconsistent customs valuation and the use of minimum import prices, which may be applied arbitrarily to calculate customs duties.

WTO Information Technology Agreement

The United States has expressed concerns about EU proposals to apply duties as high as 14 percent to imports of several technologically-sophisticated versions of products covered under the WTO Information Technology Agreement (ITA). Such products include certain set-top boxes with a communication function (e.g. cable boxes), flat panel displays for computers, digital still image video cameras, and certain units of automatic data processing machines (e.g. multifunction or "all-in-one" printer/copier/scanner devices). All ITA Members, including the EU, committed to bind and eliminate customs duties on these products when coverage for the ITA was finalized in 1996. However, the EU continued to draft proposals in 2006 that would redefine what products are eligible for duty-free treatment, limiting such treatment to less technologically sophisticated versions of these products, many of which are no longer sold in today's marketplace. These new product definitions proposed by the EU are not found in the ITA and are so narrow that almost none of today's models of the aforementioned ITA products would be guaranteed duty-free treatment if imported into the EU. The United States has raised its concerns both bilaterally and in the ITA Committee in Geneva and will continue to press the EU to abide by the letter and spirit of the ITA.

Restrictions Affecting U.S. Wine Exports

Since the mid-1980s, U.S. wines have been permitted entry to the EU market through temporary exemptions from certain EU wine regulations governing permissible wine-making practices. The temporary nature of these derogations created continuous uncertainty for U.S. wine exporters. In 2002, the EU adopted a new wine labeling regulation (Commission Regulation No. 753/2002). The United States, along with a number of other WTO Members, raised serious concerns about the lack of clarity in the new regulation and its WTO-consistency and urged the EU to withdraw the regulation. The regulation appeared to be more trade restrictive than necessary to meet any legitimate objective, as it would prohibit the presentation on imported wine of information important for the marketing of wine unless certain conditions were met (e.g., the marketing information used must be regulated in the producing country). In addition, the EU imposed restrictions on the use of traditional terms listed in the regulation, in some instances granting exclusive use of a term to an EU wine, thereby raising national treatment concerns. Traditional terms are, for the most part, terms used with certain other expressions (often geographical indications) to describe wine or liqueur and in many cases the terms are merely descriptive (e.g., "ruby" and "tawny").

On March 10, 2006, the European Union and the United States signed an agreement on certain aspects of wine trade as a first phase to a broader agreement on trade in wine. The agreement, which went into effect the day of the signing, is intended to eliminate the uncertainties caused by the previous temporary exemptions and to provide more stable market conditions for the wine sector. The pact simplifies export procedures for American wine-makers hoping to increase their share of a trade currently worth around $2.8 billion annually. It provides for mutual acceptance of current wine-making practices and sets up a consultative process for accepting new wine-making practices. It also addresses some of the concerns raised by the EU's wine-labeling regulation, including a provision for the use of certain EU-regulated terms on U.S. wine. Finally, the agreement provides for the negotiation of an additional agreement to further facilitate trade in wine between the parties. These negotiations began in June 2006.

Bananas

Acting against the backdrop of understandings reached separately with the United States and Ecuador in 2001 setting out the means for reaching a resolution to the long-running dispute regarding trade in bananas, the EU instituted a new banana import regime on January 1, 2006. The 2001 understandings required that by January 1, 2006, the EU must put in place a tariff-only regime for bananas. The understandings further required the EU to seek waivers of its GATT Article I and XIII obligations in order to continue temporarily a modified banana import regime incorporating tariff-rate quotas and import licensing requirements. The Article I waiver as finally granted by the WTO required that the future tariff-only regime result in at least maintaining total market access for MFN banana suppliers.

In the fall of 2005, the EU made two proposals for a new tariff rate for bananas. Both of these proposals were subject to review by a WTO arbitrator (according to the terms of the Article I waiver), which found that both proposals failed to satisfy the EU's obligation at least to maintain total market access for non-preferential suppliers of bananas to the EU market. EU consultations and negotiations with a number of Latin American banana exporting countries throughout 2005 yielded no agreement on the shape of the EC's post-January 1, 2006 regime. The regime as eventually implemented on January 1, 2006, combined a 176 euro/metric ton most-favored nation (MFN) tariff level with a continued zero duty tariff-rate quota for bananas originating in Africa, Pacific and Caribbean (ACP) countries, with whom the EU maintains a preferential trading relationship. In November 2006, after continued negotiations failed to achieve a satisfactory result, Ecuador filed a request under Article 21.5 of the WTO Dispute Settlement Understanding for consultations with the EU regarding the compliance of this new regime with the EU's obligations under the WTO. The United States joined as a third party in these consultations.

The United States' strong interest is that the EU's import regime must uphold the EU's multilateral commitment to put in place a WTO-compatible structure that at least maintains total market access for non-preferential banana suppliers. While the United States does not directly export bananas to the EU, this is an issue of considerable importance to U.S. companies involved in the production, distribution, and marketing of bananas.

Market Access Restrictions for U.S. Pharmaceuticals

U.S. pharmaceutical companies encounter persistent market access problems throughout countries of the European Union due to the effective price, volume, and access controls placed on medicines by national governments. In most cases, Member State governments administer medicine reimbursement programs as part of their healthcare programs, which cover a significant segment of the market. The procedures for getting a product on the reimbursement list and the price controls maintained for those products that are on the list lack transparency and have a strong negative impact on U.S. exports. The EU also places strict controls on the nature of information that pharmaceutical companies can furnish to patients. The combination of these measures can limit patients' access to innovative products and may diminish investments by EU companies in pharmaceuticals research and development.

The EU's single market allows pharmaceuticals, like other goods, to move freely within the EU, while Member States' controlled prices vary greatly from one country to another. This situation permits intermediaries to buy medicines, often in bulk quantities, in EU countries where the government-determined price is lower and sell them in other EU countries where the price is set at a higher level – a practice known as parallel trade, where traders do not contribute any value to research and development costs.

Austria

Austria maintains a bureaucratic pharmaceutical reimbursement approval process that limits market access for innovative products. A pharmaceutical firm seeking to include a product on the list of reimbursable drugs without prior authorization must first obtain the approval of the umbrella organization of social insurance funds (Hauptverband/HVB). Almost all new innovative pharmaceuticals must be individually approved by HVB physicians, who remain reluctant to prescribe them to avoid bureaucratic hurdles. A reform of the reimbursement system came into effect on January 1, 2005, but the situation has not improved. U.S. companies operating in Austria report cumulative losses between $25 million and $100 million due to these practices.

Belgium

Pharmaceutical companies consider Belgium among the most inhospitable markets in Europe. Taxes, pricing policies, and slow approvals discourage investment in research and development. Prices on pharmaceuticals reimbursed through the Belgian healthcare system remain at well below European averages, and there is strong government pressure on doctors to favor generics and lowest-cost drugs over patented products. Further, in addition to the turnover and profit taxes applied exclusively in this sector, pharmaceutical companies are required to fund a buffer to cover what have been chronic gaps between budgeted and actual government spending on pharmaceuticals. In combination, these tax measures amount to a 10 percent to 11 percent additional levy on the sector. The government did not pass promised legislation in 2006 to exempt drugs under patent from a mandatory price decrease that went into effect in the fall of 2005.

Bulgaria

The Bulgarian government's drug supply mechanism constitutes a major market access barrier to U.S. pharmaceutical exports. New drug legislation imposes liability on companies for failures of distributors to meet drug supply obligations (incorrect or late deliveries). Instead of holding distributors accountable for correct distribution, the government holds pharmaceutical manufacturers liable for the distributors' performance, over which manufacturers have no control. The registration processes for pharmaceutical products and for drug pricing and reimbursement, including the process by which the National Health Insurance Fund classifies drugs, are cumbersome and non-transparent. Newer drugs are often arbitrarily classified with their older, generic versions for pricing purposes, thereby limiting companies' ability to recover their research and development costs.

Cyprus

The Cypriot pharmaceuticals market suffers from several distortions that have resulted in unnecessary barriers to trade and retail shortages of many pharmaceuticals. Of the 3,300 drugs sold in Cyprus prior to May 1, 2004, only around 2000 were available in October 2006.

Since acceding to the EU on May 1, 2004, the government of Cyprus (GOC) imposed retail price cuts for pharmaceuticals of around 20 percent. The mechanism used by the GOC to set pharmaceutical retail prices involves using a basket of prices of the same drug in eight other EU countries (identified as two high price, four medium price, and two low price countries). However, local representatives of pharmaceutical companies believe the selected countries are not representative, pushing the benchmark price downward. During 2006, the situation improved somewhat, with marginal price concessions to pharmaceutical importers.

Furthermore, the government discriminates against new, innovative drugs when procuring pharmaceuticals for the public health sector. Innovative, cutting-edge drugs are generally left off the government's procurement list until cheaper substitutes become available. Cyprus is currently overhauling its national health scheme, aiming to upgrade public health care by 2008. The process may result in reforms to the current government procurement system.

Czech Republic

In October 2005, the European Commission sent a letter initiating infringement proceedings against the government of the Czech Republic for not properly implementing the EU Transparency Directive. The complaint focused on the non-transparent pharmaceutical categorization process that decides which medicines will be covered by public health insurance and determines the level of reimbursement. In October 2006, the EC alerted the GOCR that they would move toward potential legal action unless the GOCR corrects this lack of transparency. The GOCR has drafted a legislative plan in consultation with industry and the EC to address the issue.

Denmark

The pharmaceutical industry, in general, and U.S. firms in particular, complain that Danish reimbursement standards lack objective and verifiable criteria and do not meet even minimal standards of transparency. Furthermore, the industry claims that the Danish government has failed to provide reimbursement for new innovative medicines or has delayed reimbursement for long periods. Within the context of the Danish social security system, this has the practical effect of preventing the sale and use of such medicines. The government has maintained pressure to further decrease prices or sales of innovative pharmaceutical products, and as of April 1, 2005, a new reimbursement system was introduced. Under the new rules, reimbursements are determined on the basis of the lowest-priced medicine available in each therapeutic category, meaning that the patients' own contributions increase unless the cheapest product (often generics) is chosen. Reimbursements only apply to medicines bought in a Danish-authorized pharmacy.

Finland

Innovative pharmaceutical companies in Finland have raised concerns that government regulations have resulted in an uncompetitive environment marked by pricing policies that place low ceilings on pharmaceutical prices and limit the price differentials allowed between generic and innovative products. Further, industry claims that it takes more than three years for a pharmaceutical product to be approved for full reimbursement under the national insurance scheme.

In early 2004, Finland's Ministry of Social Affairs and Health (MoSAH) began preparing legislation that would extend the time that brand-name drugs are protected from competition by generic alternatives. Research-based pharmaceutical companies, legislators and civil servants at MoSAH and the Ministry of Trade and Industry worked closely together and produced a report to the Minister of Social Affairs and Health. Parliament approved an amendment to the Finnish Medicine Act in late 2005 that prevents the inclusion of patent-infringing generic pharmaceuticals on national mandatory generic substitution lists. This amendment entered into effect on February 1, 2006.

France

France's new Health High Authority, HAS ("Haute Autorite de Sante"), an advisory body set up by the French government to spur French healthcare reform, began its activities on January 1, 2005. HAS plays a critical role in assessing the expected or actual clinical benefit delivered by healthcare products, procedures and services, and advises on decisions about inclusion of a product, medical device, health technology or procedure on the list of products and services that qualify for reimbursement under the French Social Security system. Since its inception, HAS has recommended that 221 drugs be removed from the list of reimbursable drugs. In spite of complaints from pharmaceutical companies, the new agency confirmed that France would maintain its own, separate assessment of innovative drugs, even after these products have been granted a Marketing Authorization under the Centralized European Procedure. HAS notes that the specific features of the French healthcare environment will have to be taken into account but that France intends, where possible, to initiate a strategy of alliances with other similar healthcare bodies in the EU.

Germany

As part of a broader health-care reform package, Germany introduced a reference pricing scheme on generic and patented pharmaceuticals on January 1, 2005. U.S. firms contend that they bear the brunt of cost-containment by virtue of their dominance (25 percent) of the German market. U.S. pharmaceutical companies note serious concerns about lack of transparency and fairness in the decision-making process related to the new reference pricing scheme, which does not provide a fair rate of return for patented, innovative medicines. Additional cost constraint measures were imposed through the combining of patented, innovative products with generic products, known as "jumbo groups." Both reference pricing and its variant, jumbo groups, are strongly opposed by U.S. pharmaceutical companies. The U.S. Government has raised this issue repeatedly with the German government, including during the visits of interagency U.S. health policy delegations to Berlin in June 2005 and February 2006. Legislation that went into effect in May 2006 clarified how drugs are declared innovative and provided more transparency in the decision-making process, addressing some industry concerns. The German government has continued to debate new, broader healthcare reform legislation, but the packages put forward to date have not contained further measures that would alleviate the disadvantages to U.S. and other countries' producers of innovative pharmaceuticals.

Hungary

In June 2004, the Hungarian government and various pharmaceutical companies signed a contract to end price freezes until December 31, 2006 and return drug prices to March 2004 levels. In addition, a draft document by the State Reform Committee suggests that healthcare spending could remain at current levels until 2010, in effect extending a June 2004 agreement that limits health budget increases to 5 percent. This measure, in conjunction with an October 2005 cap on company payments to the health budget, could have negative results for drug manufacturers, since current regulations state that pharmaceutical companies are responsible for financing gaps in the drug subsidy budget. Finally, the government of Hungary initiated a generic drug program in June 2005 encouraging doctors to prescribe alternatives to the name brands as part of its "100 steps" program.

Italy

U.S. companies have raised concerns about Italian government measures that they believe will have a deleterious impact on their business and could have a negative impact on patient care. Among these are: (i) an across-the-board decrease in reimbursement prices for almost 300 drugs now on the reimbursement list; (ii) an increase in the amount that industry must "pay back" to the central government for regions' annualized overspending on pharmaceuticals; and (iii) additional discounts on certain classes of drugs that will disproportionately disadvantage

U.S. research-based companies. U.S. companies are eager to continue a dialogue with the Italian government to improve transparency in Italy's cost-containment measures and look for solutions that provide the greatest value in terms of potentially lifesaving innovation and patient care.

Lithuania

Some pharmaceutical products in Lithuania are sold at very low prices to consumers. The government reimburses pharmaceutical manufacturers the difference between this price and a price set by the health insurance law. The Lithuanian government amended this law on July 5, 2005, to change the formula used to calculate this price. The new formula yields a price that is 5 percent less than the average price of the drug in six Central and Eastern European countries. Pharmaceutical manufacturers are not required to participate in this system, and outside of this system, they are free to market their products and charge market prices.

The Netherlands

The Dutch Ministry of Health views pharmaceuticals as a prime target for savings in its national healthcare budget. Industry asserts that the Ministry does not fully recognize the added value of incremental innovation. Various measures are in force or planned that delay the reimbursement of new compounds or favor generic drugs. The current multi-party agreement between the Ministry of Health, insurers, pharmacists, and generic manufacturers was extended for another year in 2005. Nefarma, the association representing the innovative industry, joined the agreement on January 1, 2005. Under the current agreement, Nefarma members will reduce their prices of multi-source brands (out-of-patent products for which there are generics available) by an average of 40 percent. This reduction affects older products, while new, innovative products are protected. Discussions among the same stakeholders now have the objective of either extending the multi-party agreement after the end of 2007 or to modernize the current reimbursement system and/or the Pharmaceutical Pricing Act.

Poland

For several years, the Polish government has alleged that foreign pharmaceutical companies charged excessive margins for drugs and owed hundreds of millions of dollars in fines under a 2000-2002 ordinance related to pharmaceutical pricing. Although this ordinance was subsequently struck down by Polish courts, the issue remains unsettled and subject to potential legal action by both the National Health Fund and Finance Ministry. Poland has thus far ignored requests for EU arbitration of this issue. The uncertainty and amount of the potential fines threaten not only future investment, but also the existing investments of foreign innovative pharmaceutical firms in Poland.

In July 2006, the Polish government instituted a 13 percent across-the-board price cut on all imported pharmaceutical products. The Polish government contended that it cut prices in response to exchange rate changes. According to the U.S. pharmaceutical industry, however, the Polish government makes reimbursements in Polish zloty and should therefore be unaffected by exchange rate variations. The pharmaceutical industry has also raised questions of WTO-consistency, on the grounds that the regulation applies only to importers. The European Commission is investigating the consistency of the price reductions with EU rules. In September 2006, some foreign pharmaceutical companies were issued additional price reductions to hospital supply products ranging from 4 percent to 34 percent that entered into effect in early October 2006. No explanation was given for the reductions.

Polish legislation requires that the Ministry of Health update its drug reimbursement list at least once a year. It is from this list that doctors most often prescribe drugs as purchases are subsidized by the Polish National Health Fund, making them more affordable for patients. In the seven years prior to December 2006, the Polish Ministry of Health added only four innovative drugs to its reimbursement list. Failure to add drugs to the reimbursement list seriously undermined U.S. and international innovative drug producers' market position in favor of the Polish generic industry. In December of 2006, the Health Ministry added 12 new innovative drugs to its reimbursement list (comprising over 50 products). The Polish government announced that it plans to add another 20 innovative drugs (comprising over 100 products) to the list in Summer 2007. The U.S. pharmaceutical industry is concerned that reimbursement prices are set arbitrarily and often without transparency. Pending legislation will require the Health Ministry to publish its selection criteria and formalize an appeals process for drugs not selected for the reimbursement list.

Portugal

In September 2006, Portugal enacted the Consumption of Medicine in Hospitals statute, an adaptation of EU Directive 2004/27/EC. The statute restricts the introduction of new medicines in hospitals, with the exception of generics, by requiring studies demonstrating that the new drugs are more cost effective than the generic versions. An individual study can cost up to $50,000 and take one year to complete. This restriction already existed for new entries in the retail sector. Industry estimates that these requirements will result in a cost to U.S. firms of $315,000 in studies and $12.6 million in lost sales.

Pharmaceuticals destined for retail and hospital use have been given 0 percent and 4 percent growth ceilings, respectively. If the pharmaceutical industry surpasses these percentages, it will be required to repay the government the overage, not to exceed $30 million and $15 million, respectively.

Substantial delays in government payments to the pharmaceutical industry persist although the government's outstanding debt has decreased from $1 billion in 2005 to $883 million in 2006.

Spain

A pharmaceutical must go through a lengthy and costly approval and registration process with the Spanish Ministry of Health unless it was previously registered in another EU Member State or with the European Medicines Agency. This process delays the entry of innovative pharmaceuticals into the Spanish market. Further delays are caused by a lengthy administrative pricing process, coupled with onerous government reimbursement procedures.

Slovakia

U.S. and European pharmaceutical companies complain that a Slovakian Ministry of Health decree (No. 723/2004), which went into effect on October 15, 2005, further reduces the transparency of government decisions regarding the pricing and reimbursement decisions for medicines prescribed by national health insurance. The decree specifies the rules to be applied in determining the price of the medicinal product and level of reimbursement. The original decree provided detailed rules for the calculation of the price and the level of reimbursement. However, recent amendment of the decree cancelled the detailed rules for determining the reimbursement amount and, instead, provided the Ministry of Health, as the deciding authority, with wide discretion to decide on the amount of reimbursement without setting a clear set of guidelines for such decisions. All parameters on the list are reviewable by the Ministry of Health four times a year. Since these decisions fall outside the Slovak Administrative Code, there is no formal process for the decisions to be appealed by the companies. The new regulation has increased the subjectivity of the Board's decision-making, thereby minimizing the predictability and transparency of the process.

Slovenia

Non-Slovene pharmaceutical companies have expressed concern about the government of Slovenia's non-transparent procedures in pricing and reimbursement. In November 2005, the government moved to implement Therapeutic Reference Pricing (TRP), most likely as an attempt at reducing government expenditures. Pharmaceutical stakeholders have claimed that this penalizes innovation while rewarding imitation. Through proactive measures by innovative companies, TRP was left out of the New Medicine Law. The threat of TRP continues and will continue as the government of Slovenia tries to reduce government spending on health without enacting measures unpopular with citizens.

Innovative U.S. drug manufacturers continue to face pricing issues, with the government setting price limitations based on a "basket" of "European average prices." Currently, the government is considering an option to match its price to the lowest price in the "basket" rather than the average, threatening to further inhibit Slovenian consumers' access to new drugs. Slovenian regulations require health professionals to prescribe drugs with the lowest price in their group as stated on the Interchangeable Drug List (IDL). These are the only drugs that are fully reimbursed under the state insurance plan.

United Kingdom (UK)

The UK's National Institute for Health and Clinical Excellence (NICE) is responsible for judging the clinical and cost-effectiveness of new and existing drugs, treatments, and medical devices, and providing guidance to the UK's National Health Service (NHS) on whether the NHS should fund a treatment. NICE's review is in addition to the normal national approval process through the

UK's Medicines and Healthcare Products Regulatory Agency. The slow implementation and lack of transparency of NICE guidance is a disincentive for U.S. and European pharmaceutical companies to launch innovative products in the UK.

The UK also limits the profits pharmaceutical companies are allowed on their sales to NHS through the Pharmaceutical Price Regulation Scheme (PPRS), which requires companies that sold more than $2 million worth of branded medicines to the NHS in the previous year to reduce prices by 7 percent. Companies that exceed the profit target by more than 40 percent must refund the excess either as a lump sum payment to the Department of Health or as price reductions to the NHS. The Office of Fair Trading has recommended replacing the PPRS with a value-based pricing system.

Uranium Imports

The United States is concerned that EU policies may restrict the import into the EU of enriched uranium and possibly downstream goods such as nuclear fuel, nuclear rods, and assemblies. Since 1992, the EU has maintained strict quantitative restrictions on imports of enriched uranium to protect its domestic producers. Since 1994, these restrictions have been applied in accordance with the terms of the Corfu Declaration, a joint European Council and European Commission policy statement that has never been made public or notified to the WTO. The Corfu Declaration appears to impose explicit quotas on imports of enriched uranium, limiting imports to only about 20 percent of the European market. The United States has raised concerns about the import quotas and the non-transparent nature of the Corfu Declaration and its application. Further, the United States is closely monitoring whether future EU agreements with Russia under negotiation in the nuclear area will follow WTO rules on import quotas and transparency.

Chapter 3

STANDARDS, TESTING, LABELING AND CERTIFICATION

OVERVIEW

With the decline of traditional transatlantic trade barriers, EU regulatory measures are increasingly viewed as impediments for U.S. exporters of manufactured and agricultural products. Compliance with divergent technical regulations and standards for products sold in the United States and the EU imposes additional costs on U.S. exporters (e.g., duplicative testing, product redesign) and increases the time required to bring a product to market. Such costs for U.S. exporters are compounded by a lack of transparency in the development of EU regulations and a lack of meaningful opportunity for non-EU stakeholders to provide input on draft EU regulations and standards. To address these systemic concerns, the United States continues to promote greater U.S.-EU regulatory cooperation and enhanced transparency in the EU regulatory system.

Despite often sharing similar regulatory objectives, the U.S.-EU dialogue frequently is unable to promptly resolve regulatory-based trade problems. In particular, many U.S. exporters view the EU's growing use of its "precautionary principle" to restrict or prohibit trade in certain products, in the absence of a scientific justification for doing so, as a pretext for market protection. Further, EU regulatory barriers are often compounded by multiple and overlapping measures affecting particular products. Poultry, beef, agricultural biotechnology products, and wine are examples of products that face multiple layers of restrictive regulation in the EU marketplace. To illustrate:

- U.S. efforts to reopen the EU to U.S. poultry exports have been hindered by multiple obstacles. As a result, resolution of any one obstacle (e.g., the EU allowing the use of alternative antimicrobial treatments on poultry meat) would not necessarily result in a reopening of trade due to the existence of other obstacles (such as requirements regarding on-farm practices for raising poultry). Beef trade faces similar problems.
- U.S. exporters of agricultural biotechnology products have been harmed not only by the *de facto* moratorium on approving new products but also by the existence of certain Member State prohibitions on products already approved for marketing within the European Community. This was the subject of a successful WTO challenge by the United States.
- Despite the recent conclusion of a U.S.-EU agreement on wine trade, U.S. wine exporters are still confronted by the uncertainty surrounding the EU's restrictions on labeling practices, as well as high tariffs, heavy subsidization of EU wine producers, uneven recognition of wine labels at the Member State level, failure to provide protection for foreign GIs, and public affairs campaigns denigrating the quality of U.S. wine.

STANDARDIZATION

Given the massive U.S.-EU trade relationship and the volume of EU standardization work in regulated market segments, European standards activities are of considerable importance to U.S. exporters. A number of standards-related problems continue to impede U.S. exports, including a general inability to participate in the formation of EU standards and occasional reliance on design-based, rather than performance-based, standards. Disparities between the practices of some European conformity assessment bodies add to the frustration and cost for American exporters. In addition, there are concerns related to the procedures, responsibilities (e.g., accountability and redress), and lack of transparency in the Member States, the European Commission, and the European standards bodies. In the case of many sectors, European directives and their relevant standards pose a significant impediment to American exports.

Pressure Equipment

In May 2002, the EU Pressure Equipment Directive (PED) entered into force, imposing new requirements on manufacturers of such equipment. Previously, pressure equipment manufacturers could demonstrate conformity based on standards for material specifications, including the

U.S. ASME Code. Manufacturers using the ASME Code may now be excluded from the EU market because the European standards incorporate material specifications slightly different from those found in the ASME Code. In the absence of a full set of harmonized EU standards, the PED permits manufacturers to file for an EAM (European Approval of Materials); however, few requests for EAMs have been approved so far. Another option, the Particular Material Appraisal (PMA), is a costly process for which there are no clearly defined procedures in the PED. In light of these factors, U.S. manufacturers seek continued acceptance of materials that meet the ASME code that have been widely used in Europe for decades prior to the PED. In an effort to bring the two sides closer together, U.S. and EU officials and stakeholders agreed to a pilot project to eliminate redundant testing requirements for materials. The two sides are beginning technical cooperation, starting with an attempt to harmonize several testing standards.

The Netherlands

The Dutch parliament has shelved consideration of a proposed amendment to the Environmental Management Act that could have significantly impacted U.S. exporters of wood products. The amendment would have required assessment criteria to be equivalent to one particular certification program to the exclusion of others, require a declaration on where the wood is produced, as well as an auditor's report of delivery. The amendment was shelved following an agreement between the Dutch government, wood industry, and NGOs on a certifying system to test sustainable produced wood.

Agricultural Biotechnology Products

Since 1998, the European Union's Council of Ministers has not managed to assemble a qualified majority of EU Member States in support of agricultural biotechnology product approvals, despite the lack of any legitimate health or safety reason not to approve them. While the European Commission granted approval for a limited number of biotechnology products under its legislative authority, the United States considers that the EU continues to lack a predictable, workable process for approving these products in a way that reflects scientific, rather than political factors. At the level of the EU Council, it is clear that many Member States still actively support and maintain a *de facto* moratorium on product approvals.

In May 2003, the United States initiated a WTO dispute settlement process related to the EU's *de facto* moratorium on approvals of biotechnology products and to the existence of individual Member State marketing prohibitions on previously approved biotechnology products. The panel hearing this dispute delivered its interim report in February 2006 and published the final report on September 29. The European Commission has not yet indicated how it plans to implement the panel report.

Several Member States have imposed marketing bans (safeguard measures) on some biotechnology products that had been previously approved at the EU level. On June 24, 2005, the Environment Council rejected, by a qualified majority, the eight Commission proposals to lift safeguard measures imposed by five Member States against biotechnology maize. On October 5, 2005, the European Court of Justice ruled against Upper Austria's effective ban on growing biotechnology crops since there was no scientific evidence to substantiate the ban.

Recent public attacks on the EU's independent scientific authority, the European Food Safety Authority (EFSA), appear to be slowing down the approval process. Specifically, the European Commission published a proposal on April 12 on improving the agriculture biotechnology legislative framework that has been implemented retroactively on EFSA biotechnology food safety opinions. In 2006, the Austrian EU Presidency presided over the debate on EFSA and also attempted to revise decision-making criteria for biotechnology approvals, despite the fact that the Member States had approved the decision-making procedure presently in place. The Environment Council did push the Commission to revisit criteria for EFSA scientific opinions; this could create further undue delays of biotechnology product approvals.

On August 18, 2006, USDA announced that a biotechnology rice variety (LL 601) had been detected in samples taken from U.S. long grain rice. At that time, LL601 was not approved for marketing in either the EU or the United States, but has since been deregulated in the United States. While both the EU and the United States have reviewed the available scientific data and concluded that there are no human health, food safety, or environmental concerns associated with this rice, the DG for Health and Consumer Protection (DG SANCO) directed the 25 Member States to test products for the presence of LL 601 rice in their markets. Trace elements were found in both bulk shipments and in processed food products, resulting in product rejection and destruction. However, differences in testing protocols on both sides of the Atlantic raised questions about the reliability of testing. In response, the U.S. Government began intensive talks with EU officials to establish a common protocol for bulk shipments from the United States in an effort to avoid mandatory testing upon arrival in the EU. These talks failed to produce an agreement and the Commission, with Member State support, introduced mandatory testing at destination, effective October 23, 2006. This has had the effect of continuing the effective embargo on trade in rice from the United States.

Co-Existence

In accordance with the European Commission's guidance document on the co-existence of biotechnology and conventional crops, which recommends a regional approach to co-existence issues, a number of Member States (including Spain, Denmark, Germany, Italy, the Netherlands and most regions in Austria) have drafted new co-existence laws or have chosen to provide industry guidance. While the decrees/laws vary substantially from country to country, they generally require extensive control, monitoring and reporting of biotechnology crops. The European Commission may initiate infringement proceedings against a Member State's co-existence law if it is judged to be incompatible with EU law. However, there is no time limit on how quickly the Commission must act. The European Commission and the Austrian EU Presidency co- hosted a Conference on Co-existence in April 2006. In addition to the Conference's conclusion that there was a need for all Member States to define their co-existence policy, there was a call for a European-wide seed threshold to assist governments in choosing scientifically-based separation distances.

Traceability and Labeling

In April 2004, EC Regulations 1829/2003 and 1830/2003 governing the approval, traceability and labeling of biotechnology food and feed became effective. The regulations include mandatory traceability and labeling for all biotechnology and downstream products. Among the traceability rules are requirements that information that a product contains or consists of biotechnology products must be transmitted to each operator throughout the entire supply chain. Operators must also have a standardized system in place to keep information about biotechnology products and to identify the operator by whom and to whom it was transferred for a period of five years from each transaction. The requirements include an obligation to label appropriate products and to indicate if the food is different from its conventional counterpart in composition, nutritional value, intended use or health implications.

In some cases, these burdensome directives have already severely restricted market access for U.S. food suppliers because food producers have reformulated their products to eliminate the use of biotechnology products. Food producers have indicated concern about needing to find expensive or limited alternatives. The Directives generally are anticipated to have a negative impact on a wide range of U.S. exports, including processed food exports. The European Commission issued a report in spring 2006 on the implementation of the traceability and labeling directive that was largely inconclusive because of the limited number of products containing biotechnology material that have entered the EU market.

Austria

The Austrian Biotechnology Law allows, in principle, for planting of biotechnology crops. However, strict and complicated rules on liability and compensation still represent a *de facto* barrier against all EU-approved biotechnology crops. All nine Austrian provinces have passed biotechnology precautionary bills to protect their organic and small-scale agricultural sector. Three Austrian ordinances still ban the planting of all EU-approved biotechnology crops and a new fourth ordinance bans the marketing of a biotechnology oilseed rape. Under current Austrian rules, unapproved biotechnology events must not be detected in conventional seeds ("zero tolerance"), but EU-approved events may be present in conventional and organic seeds up to 0.1 percent.

Driven by political rather than scientific factors, the government of Austria has effectively banned most agricultural biotechnology applications apart from research. All major Austrian supermarket chains have banned biotechnology products from their shelves, even those labeled according to EC regulations.

Baltic Countries

In Estonia, Latvia, and Lithuania, the scientific community in each country broadly agrees that the technology is safe and can provide benefits to producers and consumers. Some officials in Estonia and Latvia have expressed interest in the potential use of biotechnology for industrial purposes, such as the production of paper from high-starch potatoes and cellulosic biofuel from willows and grasses.

Despite concerns, all three countries are moving forward with developing co-existence regulations and agreed to a general framework for such regulations in July 2006. The proposed documentation and registration requirements for farmers wishing to plant biotechnology seed are quite onerous in each of the country's draft proposals. Currently, interest in biotechnology among Baltic farmers does not seem high, because the region's climate is less favorable for the biotechnology seed varieties currently approved in the EU. New seed varieties could stimulate interest, but onerous co-existence requirements could slow or even stifle use.

Cyprus

Cyprus has adopted increasingly tough standards for biotechnology products, which, in some cases, exceed minimum EU requirements. For example: (a) GOC application requirements for new agricultural biotechnology crops are more arduous than in other EU countries; (b) permits for such crops must be renewed every five years; and (c) the GOC has declared as "GMO-free" areas under the Natura 2000 project (corresponding to 14 percent of Cyprus). Biotechnology products that are already licensed in the EU may circulate in Cyprus freely. However, biotechnology organisms must be approved, even if they are already licensed in other EU countries.

France

A biotechnology bill transposing EU Directives 1998/81 and 2001/18, which provides for coexistence measures, and revises the regulatory approval process for France, passed the Senate in March 2006 but has not been considered by the National Assembly. It is unlikely that the bill will proceed further in the legislative process before the May 2007 national elections. The French government will be required to pay penalties to the European Commission (EC) if the Directives 1998/91 and 2001/18 are not transposed on time. Notwithstanding the lack of co-existence regulations in France, biotechnology corn production increased from 500 hectares in 2005 to 5,000 hectares in 2006. France has consistently entertained applications for biotechnology research plots and accepted 30 applications for research in open-fields in 2006. In addition, since

2004, France has, at the EU level, voted in favor of certain biotechnology products under Directive 2001/18.

In 2005 and 2006, anti-biotechnology activists destroyed more than 50 percent of test fields in France and recently attacked several commercial biotechnology corn fields. The French Ministry of Agriculture issued two press communiques this summer condemning the destruction of research and commercial crops that are produced legally in France. The communiques were particularly noteworthy, since before these incidents, the Ministry did not have a strong track record of condemning such behavior. Agriculture Minister Bussereau affirmed his support to farmers and researchers stating that firm instructions had been given to local authorities to guarantee the security of biotechnology test plots and that legal proceedings will be launched systematically against those who destroy biotechnology crops.

Germany

In November 2005, the new grand coalition government decided to re-examine the biotechnology law with the goal of making the legal rules for biotechnology crops more practicable. As of November 2006, this had yet to occur because of the lack of consensus on several key points, including liability. Also in November 2005, Germany approved five Bt corn varieties for commercial planting. In 2006, farmers mainly in eastern Germany planted 950 hectares of Bt corn compared to about 300 hectares in 2005. The seed industry is optimistic that the Bt corn area will rise further in 2007. In the summer of 2006, farmers interested in biotechnology seeds founded a self-help organization for farmers interested in biotechnology crop production called InnoPlanta AGIL which has carried out several outreach and educational activities. Despite these positive developments, the number of vandalistic field destructions increased in 2006.

Greece

Greece has opposed the introduction of biotechnology seeds for field tests, despite support for such tests by Greek farmers and Greece's agricultural science community.

Hungary

Extensive biotechnology research is taking place in Hungary, and the Hungarian government has allowed field tests for herbicide resistant corn, wheat and other crops. Although Hungary is required to adopt all relevant EU biotechnology legislation, Hungary has not yet prepared the national application rules for the EU biotechnology regulations on food and feed, and traceability and labeling. In early 2007, the EU Council again upheld Hungary's "safeguard clause" and with it a January 2005 Hungarian moratorium on corn varieties containing the Monsanto MON 810 event. The measure bans the production, use, distribution, and import of hybrids deriving from the MON 810 maize lines. The ban applies to seed producers and distributors as well as farmers. The moratorium is being addressed in the context of the country's co-existence legislation, which is currently awaiting Parliamentary approval and serves as the regulatory framework through which Hungary views biotechnology in the agricultural sector.

Italy

There are varying positions on agricultural biotechnology products among Italy's Ministries of Health, Agriculture, and Environment. The Ministry of Agriculture has imposed rigorous thresholds for seed purity in an effort to minimize the risk of adventitious presence. Current regulations permit only the minimum detectable 0.05 percent of biotechnology seeds to be present. In the case of soybeans used for animal feed, the Ministry of Agriculture allows the use of imported biotechnology beans, as the Ministry is unable to meet Italian feed demand from non-biotechnology sources.

On November 29, 2004, the Regional Administrative Tribunal (TAR) of Lazio (which includes Rome) annulled the decree banning the commercialization of four EU-approved biotechnology corn varieties (BT11, MON 810, MON 809, and T25). Separately, in March 2006, the Italian High Court ruled that coexistence legislation enacted by Parliament was unconstitutional. In its ruling, the Court stated that Italy's regions are responsible for the development of co-existence legislation. The regions are engaged in this task, although only a few are expected to consider the interest of farmers in the process. The United States is concerned that this legislation could discourage biotechnology crop planting and will watch developments closely.

Luxembourg

Luxembourg remains staunchly opposed to biotechnology crops, banning the marketing or growing of biotechnology crops and opposing the approval of new biotechnology products for EU use. Luxembourg acknowledges that their national ban is a problem for the EU with regard to WTO obligations (Luxembourg was one of the six member states whose bans were the subject of a WTO dispute in which the WTO dispute panel found such bans to be inconsistent with WTO rules), but the issue remains politically explosive due to highly vocal opposition. Despite the EU Commission's continued efforts in 2006 to have Luxembourg withdraw its national ban, the law remains in effect. Legislation which would regulate the growing of biotechnology crops in Luxembourg remained stalled in a parliamentary committee for a second year. However, the Luxembourg Chamber of Deputies adopted a law implementing EU directive 98/44/CE on the legal protection of biotechnological inventions of 1998.

Poland

The Polish government opposes the use of biotechnology and in mid-2006 enacted legislation that bans the sale and registration (but not planting) of biotechnology seeds. In two years, it will prohibit the production, import and sale of animal feed produced from transgenic crops.

In contrast to the government's opposition to biotechnology products, many well-respected local scientists and a number of farm groups support their use. Support among farmers is growing along with the spread of the European corn borer into Poland's western corn producing regions.

The EU has notified Polish officials that their seed ban violates EU obligations but the government remains committed to its legislation. The ban may raise WTO concerns, as WTO obligations require that sanitary and phytosanitary regulations be based on science. If the ban on biotechnology feed were to be enforced, it could have a devastating impact on Polish livestock production, especially pork and poultry.

With the exception of some animal feed sales, the United States currently has little biotechnology trade with Poland, but there is strong interest in marketing transgenic seeds in the country. Poland currently does not produce any transgenic crops, with the possible exception of minor quantities grown for research purposes. Poland annually imports about 1.5 to 2.0 MMT of soybean meal, most of which is produced from transgenic soybeans. While the majority of these imports are from Argentina, some are transshipped U.S.-origin soybeans.

Portugal

Portugal, one of only five EU countries to cultivate biotechnology crops, began planting biotechnology corn in 2005. Biotechnology crops are expected to reach 1400 hectares in 2006, twice the 2005 level. However, 2005 co-existence legislation and current proposed legislation to establish biotechnology-free areas will likely constrain further expansion of biotechnology corn.

In early 2006, the government of Portugal established the Authority for Food and Economic Safety (AFES) under the auspices of the Ministry of Economy. AFES works with the European Food Safety Authority to conduct biotechnology assessment, risk monitoring and communications.

Romania

Romania's adoption of EU legislation on biotechnology has resulted in significant change of policy regarding biotechnology. Before 2006, Romania was the largest planter of biotechnology soybeans in Europe. Despite protests from domestic producers, Romania decided to drastically limit biotechnology cultivation in 2006 and to totally ban it in 2007.

Spain

Spain remains the EU member with the largest area under biotechnology corn cultivation. However, the current government tends to take a more restrictive position with respect to agricultural biotechnology. As a result, Spain typically abstains on Commission proposals for approving biotechnology events. Moreover, Spain recently released proposed regulations that would impose 220 meter distance requirements between conventional, organic and biotechnology crops. If approved, biotechnology use is likely to decline in Spain.

BARRIERS AFFECTING TRADE IN CATTLE, BEEF, POULTRY, AND ANIMAL BY-PRODUCTS

A variety of EU measures, outlined below, have the effect of severely restricting U.S. exports of livestock products to the European Union market. The adoption of EU non-tariff barriers by Romania and Bulgaria in the process of acceding to the EU in 2006 resulted in the loss of significant markets for U.S. exports.

EU HORMONE DIRECTIVE

In 1988, the EU provisionally banned the use of substances that have a hormonal growth-promoting effect in raising food-producing animals. This action effectively banned the export to the EU of beef from cattle raised in the United States. The use of hormone implants is approved by the U.S. Food and Drug Administration and is a common practice in U.S. beef cattle production. The United States launched a formal WTO dispute settlement procedure in May 1996 challenging the EU ban. In 1999, the WTO ruled that the EU's ban was inconsistent with the WTO Agreement on the Application of Sanitary and Phytosanitary Measures (SPS Agreement) because it was not based on a scientific risk assessment, and authorized the United States to impose sanctions on EU products with an annual trade value of $116.8 million.

In September 2003, the EU announced the entry into force of an amendment (EC Directive 2003/74) to its Hormone Directive (EC Directive 96/22). The new Directive recodified the ban on the use of estradiol for growth promotion purposes and established provisional bans on the five other growth hormones included in the original EU legislation. With enforcement of this new Directive, the EU argued that it was now in compliance with the earlier WTO ruling.

At present, the United States continues to apply 100 percent duties on $116.8 million of U.S. imports from the EU. In November 2004, the EU requested WTO consultations with the United States on this matter, claiming that U.S. sanctions were no longer justified. The dispute is now before a WTO panel, which is expected to publish its findings in the spring of 2007. The United States maintains that the revised EU measure cannot be considered to implement WTO recommendations and rulings related to this matter, and that the U.S. sanctions therefore remain authorized.

Animal By-Products Legislation

In October 2002, the European Commission approved EC Regulation 1774/2002, which regulates the importation of animal by-products not fit for human consumption. The regulation went into force in May 2004. During 2003, intensive technical discussions between U.S. and EU officials successfully addressed some issues and prevented trade disruption for a significant portion (at least $300 million) of U.S. exports to the EU of animal by-products. However, it is estimated that with the publication of the final text, about $100 million of U.S. animal by-product exports to the EU remain adversely affected to some degree. In particular, the United States remains concerned about various outstanding issues for which the EU has not provided risk assessments, such as a ban on the use of dead-in-transport poultry in pet food. The U.S. exports remaining most exposed to this regulation are dry pet food, other animal protein products, and some hides and skins. It is unclear as to the regulation's overall effect on further downstream products such as certain *in vitro* diagnostic products that may use animal by-products. In October 2005, the Commission presented a report to the EU Parliament recommending amendments to EC Regulation 1774/2002. Any agreed amendments would need to be voted on by the EU Parliament. The U.S. commented extensively on this report, which was also notified to the WTO. Furthermore, the Commission organized a conference on animal by-products in Brussels on September 20, 2006, following three sessions of a Training Initiative Pilot Program which took place in June, July and August 2006. The United States used this opportunity to share with Member States the numerous problems exporters have encountered with the 1774/2002 Regulation resulting from inconsistent interpretation and implementation by Member States. The U.S. Government will continue to seek progress on this issue in the short- and mid-term. A series of other products and issues under discussion are not expected to make it through the EU legislative process for another two years.

Poultry Meat Restrictions

U.S. poultry meat exports to the EU have been banned since April 1, 1997, because U.S. poultry producers currently use washes of low-concentration anti-microbial treatments (AMTs) to reduce the level of pathogens in poultry meat production, a practice not permitted by the EU sanitary regime. In December 2005, the European Commission's Food Safety Authority completed studies of four AMTs and found them to be safe, and in February 2006, the European Commission's Health and Consumer Protection Directorate General circulated the first draft of its proposal to allow those substances to be used on poultry meat in the EU market. That draft regulation proposed to ban the use of more than one AMT and require poultry treated with AMTs to be rinsed after treatment. These two requirements are not fully consistent with U.S. production methods and will limit some U.S. exporters' ability to trade poultry to the EU under this regulation, but would nonetheless mark a lifting of the ban on U.S. poultry exports. In 2007, the United States will continue to push for a regulation allowing the use of AMTs to be finalized in the EU legislative process.

Lithuania

Lithuanian veterinary officials have started to more strictly enforce EU transshipment regulations, especially those that they interpret to apply to labeling. As a result, products with labels that do not include the language of the destination country or with labels that indicate a destination other than the actual destination may be detained. For example, Lithuanian officials recently detained a shipment of U.S. poultry with labeling in Chinese destined for Kazakhstan, even though Kazakhstan permits such imports.

Finland and Sweden

The European Commission has granted both Finland and Sweden extensions of the derogations approved in their EU accession agreements, which allow both countries to continue to enforce stricter salmonella controls and stricter border controls for live animals (quarantine) than those enforced by other EU Member States. These countries also impose strict requirements regarding the importation of fresh (including frozen) meat, ground meat, and meat preparations, (with the exception of heat-treated meat) and table eggs.

Romania and Bulgaria

The European Commission has granted some Romanian and Bulgarian domestic meat-processing facilities a transition period for adopting certain EU poultry and pork meat requirements until 2009. Imports from non-EU sources, such as the United States, however, must immediately comply with the EU requirements, creating a national treatment issue. This change has practically put an end to trade in what was previously the top U.S. agricultural export to Romania, frozen broiler chickens. U.S. pork imports have also been adversely affected. The United States has raised these national treatment concerns in the WTO Sanitary and Phytosanitary Committee.

BARRIERS AFFECTING VITAMINS AND HEALTH FOOD PRODUCTS

France: France transposed its list of permitted vitamin and mineral preparations to be added in food supplements as established in EU Directives 2002/46/EC and 2006/37/EC in March 2006. However, France adopted a decree in May 2006 to set tolerance levels and daily allowance for vitamins and minerals that are not in accordance with standards established in relevant EU Directives.

Greece

In implementing the EU Food Supplement Directive, Greece restricted the sale of protein-based meal replacement products to pharmacies and specialized stores, limiting the ability of U.S. companies to sell such products through direct sales.

Spain

Spain has restrictive practices with respect to the use of vitamins and health food products. Since March 2002, Ministry of Health inspectors have raided health food shops and removed 227 different types of health food products from the market. Although the EU passed a new Directive on dietetics, Spain maintains its restrictive policy with regard to limits in vitamin and mineral composition.

Chapter 4

EMERGING REGULATORY BARRIERS

In addition to the previously mentioned trade barriers arising from EU policies regarding standards, testing, labeling, and certification, the United States has serious concerns about the ongoing development of new regulations that would appear to have serious adverse consequences for U.S. exporters in the future. The United States is actively engaging the European Union with respect to the issues outlined below.

EU DIRECTIVE ON WOOD PACKAGING MATERIAL (WPM)

In February 2005, the EU suspended its plan to implement a new Directive on wood packaging material (WPM) that could affect up to $80 billion worth of U.S. agricultural and commercial exports to the EU that are shipped on wooden pallets or in wood packaging materials. The Directive, published by the European Commission on October 5, 2004, would place a debarking requirement, in addition to heat treatment fumigation, on WPM from the United States and other countries.

The EU Directive is more restrictive than the international standard established by the International Plant Protection Convention (IPPC), Guidelines for Regulating Wood Packaging Material in International Trade (IPSM-15). IPPC members, including the EU, approved ISPM-15 to harmonize and safeguard WPM requirements in world trade. IPPC members approved specific treatments and the marking of WPM but did not support a debarking requirement in the absence of a scientific justification. The IPPC continues to assess emerging scientific studies related to this issue. EU Member States approved a further postponement of the unilateral debarking requirement until December 2008, with a review of the issue scheduled for 2007.

CHEMICALS

In October 2003, the European Commission presented its proposal for a massive overhaul of existing EU chemicals regulation. The proposal, called REACH (Registration, Evaluation, and Authorization of Chemicals), requires all chemicals produced or imported into the EU in volumes above one ton per year (affecting approximately 30,000 chemicals) to be registered in a central database, and imposes new testing and marketing requirements. Chemicals of very high concern would need an authorization for use in the EU. This legislation could impact virtually every industrial sector, from automobiles to textiles because it regulates substances on their own, in preparations, and in products.

While the United States supports the EU's objectives of protecting human health and the environment, it questions the workability of the present approach. A risk-based approach would allow the EU to address its environmental, public health and safety priorities while avoiding the imposition of disproportionate costs, large burdens on vital substance and product manufacturers and importers, and avoid the likely adverse impacts on trade and innovation. Many of the EU's trading partners expressed similar concerns.

In December 2006, the EU reached agreement on its final regulation. REACH is to enter into force on June 1, 2007. The United States will continue to monitor closely the implementation of this EU regulation and remain engaged constructively with the EU to ensure that U.S. interests are protected.

COSMETICS

The EU's cosmetics directive calls for an EU-wide ban on animal testing within the EU for cosmetic products and an EU-wide ban on the marketing/sale of cosmetic products that have been tested on animals, whether such testing has occurred inside or outside the EU. It will prohibit the sale in the EU of

U.S. cosmetics products tested on animals as of 2009 or 2013 (depending on the type of test) or earlier if the European Community has approved an alternative testing method.

To minimize possible trade disruption, the U.S. Government and the European Commission have embarked on a joint project to develop harmonized, alternative, non-animal testing methods. The project involves cooperation between the U.S. Interagency Coordinating Committee on the Validation of Alternative Methods and the European Center for the Validation of Alternative Methods (ECVAM). The aim is to develop agreed alternative testing methods that would be submitted to the OECD process for international validation. The validation of alternative methods is a long and expensive process, taking an average of seven years. The EC is actively encouraging ECVAM to pursue alternative methods in the near term.

Waste Management (WEEE and RoHS Directives)

In January 2003, the European Union adopted two Directives in an effort to address environmental concerns related to the growing volume of waste electrical and electronic equipment. The Waste Electrical and Electronic Equipment (WEEE) Directive focuses on the collection and recycling of electrical and electronic equipment waste. The Restriction of the Use of certain Hazardous Substances (RoHS) Directive addresses restrictions on the use of certain substances in electrical and electronic equipment, such as lead, mercury, cadmium, and certain flame-retardants.

Under the WEEE Directive, producers are held individually responsible for financing the collection, treatment, and recycling of the waste arising from their new products as of August 2005. Producers have the choice of managing their waste on an individual basis or participating in a collective scheme. Waste from old products is the collective responsibility of existing producers based on their market share.

Member States were required to transpose the WEEE Directive into national law by August 13, 2004, and to implement it by August 13, 2005. Many Member States are behind in their implementation and do not have their national WEEE registration systems in place. The WEEE Directive required that by December 31, 2006, Member States ensure a target of at least four kilograms of electrical and electronic equipment per inhabitant per year is being collected from private households. The policy is intended to create an incentive for companies to design more environment-friendly products.

Under the RoHS Directive, as of July 1, 2006, the placing on the European market of electrical and electronic equipment containing lead, mercury, cadmium, hexavalent chromium, polybrominated biphenyls, and polybrominated diphenyl ethers is prohibited, with some limited exemptions. The Commission Decision, published on August 18, 2005, established maximum concentration values of 0.1 percent by weight in homogenous materials for lead, mercury, hexavalent chromium, polybrominated biphenyls (PBB), and polybrominated diphenyl ethers (PDBE) and 0.01 percent by weight in homogenous materials for cadmium.

Some U.S. companies seeking to comply with the RoHS Directive claim to face significant commercial uncertainties. Firms assert that they lack sufficient, clear, and legally binding guidance from the EU on product scope and, in cases where technically viable alternatives do not exist, businesses face a lengthy, uncertain, and non-transparent exemption process. The European Commission will consider RoHS exemption requests on an ongoing basis, and will be regularly reviewing the need for existing exemptions. Some exporters claim that the uncertainty about RoHS provisions is having an adverse impact on companies as they must make practical design, production, and commercial decisions without adequate information.

Increasing the uncertainty for U.S. manufacturers is the fact that enforcement of RoHS will be managed at the national level. In the absence of a common approach to approval and established EU-wide standards and test methods, a product may be deemed compliant in one country and non-compliant in another.

Given the substantial impacts of RoHS substance bans on international trade, the U.S. Government has urged the European Commission to provide sufficiently detailed, legally binding guidance to give companies seeking to comply with RoHS commercial certainty. The United States has also urged the Commission to make the exemption process more efficient and transparent so that companies can have definitive answers more promptly on whether and how the Directive will apply to their products and to move towards greater harmonization of approaches in the implementation and enforcement of both Directives.

Battery Directive

In 2003, the European Commission proposed a revised version of the 1991 EU Battery Directive. The aim of the new Directive is to collect and recycle all waste batteries and to prevent their incineration and disposal. Producers must finance the collection, treatment, and recycling of waste batteries. On the issue of nickel cadmium (NiCd), the Commission proposes to set high collection targets rather than a ban. The impact assessment carried out by the Commission identifies this approach for dealing with NiCd batteries as the best option from the environment and economic points of view.

In July 2006, the European Parliament and the EU Council of Ministers agreed on a compromise to revise the 1991 Directive on batteries and accumulators. The new directive bans batteries containing cadmium (at levels above 0.002 percent) and mercury (at levels above 0.0005percent) but there are exceptions for emergency and alarms systems, medical equipment and cordless power tools. It also provides for collecting and recycling targets to be reached by 2016 at the latest.

Energy Using Products (EUP)

The EU framework directive promoting eco-design for energy-using products (EUP) entered into force on August 11, 2005, and EU Member States have until August 11, 2007, to transpose it into national law. Through this directive, the EU means to regulate the integration of energy efficiency and other environmental considerations at the design phase of a product. Once in place, design requirements will become legally binding for all products sold in the EU. The legislation commits the European Commission to draw up a working plan for "implementing measures" by July 2007 that will identify products and set specific standards. The directive contains an initial list of products for which technical studies are now underway, including lighting, office equipment, heating equipment, domestic appliances, air conditioning, and consumer electronics, and energy losses from standby modes. The directive sets out CE marking requirements for the items covered by implementing measures. Industry is most concerned about the possible need for a complete product life cycle analysis, and fears adverse impacts on design flexibility, new product development and introduction, as well as increased administrative burdens.

Metric Directive

Beginning January 1, 2010, the European Union Council Directive 80/181/EEC (Metric Directive) will allow the use of only metric units, and prohibit the use of any other measurements for most products sold in the EU. Going well beyond labeling, the Metric Directive will make the sole use of metric units obligatory in all aspects of life in the European Union, including on labels, packaging, advertising, catalogs, technical manuals, and user instructions. This prohibition will end a longstanding practice in the European trade community of allowing manufacturers flexibility on labeling products. When implemented, the Directive will also create an inconsistency with U.S. law. Unless the Metric Directive implementation date is extended again, as of January 1, 2010, displaying U.S. customary units on a box or label will be illegal in the EU. Most American and European companies which make consumer products will be forced to create separate labels, one for the U.S. market including both metric and imperial measurements, and another for the EU market displaying only metric units, therefore imposing additional costs.

Acceleration of the Phase-Outs of Ozone-Depleting Substances and Greenhouse Gases

As part of a wider climate change program to reduce emissions of greenhouse gases to meet its Kyoto Protocol objectives, the European Union adopted legislation in May 2006 to regulate the emission of fluorinated gases (f-gases). The measures improve the containment of f-gases and introduce specific restrictions on their marketing and use in specific applications. Two pieces of legislation were adopted – a regulation on f-gases used in stationary applications and the other, a Directive regulating hydrofluorocarbons (HFCs) in vehicle air conditioning. The first measure (the "stationary" Regulation) will impact U.S. manufacturers of stationary air conditioning and refrigeration equipment and the companies that produce the chemicals used in them. The second will affect U.S. car and parts manufacturers by phasing-out HFC134a in vehicle air conditioning beginning in 2011 with a complete ban by 2017.

The "stationary" Regulation seeks to improve containment of f-gases by setting minimum standards for inspection and recovery, and, where containment is not feasible, proposes to ban marketing and use of certain applications. Examples of applications using f-gases the Regulation seeks to ban include vehicle tires, non-refillable containers, windows, footwear, one-component foams, self-chilling drinking cans, novelty aerosols and fire extinguishers. The Regulation allows Member States to maintain or introduce stricter protective measures in order to reach Kyoto targets by December 21, 2012. The United States will continue to closely monitor Member States' implementation.

OTHER MEMBER STATE MEASURES

Some EU Member States have their own national practices regarding standards, testing, labeling, and certification. A brief discussion of the additional national practices of concern to the United States follows:

Austria

Austria became the second EU country after Denmark to ban a range of uses of the three fluorinated gases controlled under the Kyoto protocol on climate change. An ordinance that took effect on November 22, 2002, prohibits the use in new sprays, solvents, and fire extinguishers of hydrofluorocarbons (HFCs), perfluorocarbons, and sulphur hexafluoride. The ordinance phases out their use in foams between mid-2003 and the end of 2007. It bans their use in new refrigeration and air-conditioning equipment by the end of 2007. The ban appears to exempt production of HFCs in Austria for the export market. Even under the new EU regulation that focuses on containment instead of bans, the government of Austria has indicated it will try to retain its own national HFC bans.

Denmark

As of January 1, 2007, Danish law bans equipment with charges of less than 150 grams and equipment with charges over 10 kilos. Industry believes these laws will have an adverse effect on the market by creating an additional and disproportionate barrier to products that are manufactured in and distributed across the EU.

Finland

A ban on the importation and sale of new appliances containing hydrochlorofluorocarbons (HCFCs) was imposed on January 1, 2000, and remains in place. The importation of the chemical HCFC is allowed when used for maintenance of old refrigeration appliances using HCFC. New HCFC compounds used for maintenance of refrigeration equipment will be banned as of 2010 and use of all HCFC compounds, including recycled compounds, will be banned as of 2015.

Greece

Greece has not approved the use of corrugated stainless steel pipe (CSST) for use in internal gas industry applications. One U.S. company has been seeking approval to sell in the Greek market since 1997. In late 2005 the Greek standards organization, ELOT, was charged via presidential decree with developing standards for materials used in internal gas installations, which would cover CSST. As of this writing, ELOT has not yet taken the first step of forming a committee that would draft these standards.

Chapter 5

GOVERNMENT PROCUREMENT

Since the European Communities is party to the WTO Agreement on Government Procurement (GPA), all of the Member States are also subject to the GPA. This includes Romania and Bulgaria, which became subject to the GPA upon their accession to the EU in January 2007.

In an effort to open government procurement markets within the Member States, the EU in 2004 adopted a revised Utilities Directive (2004/17), covering purchases in the water, transportation, energy, and postal services sectors. Member States were mandated to implement the new Utilities Directive by the end of January 2006, but some EU Member States still had not implemented it.

This Directive requires open, objective bidding procedures but still discriminates against bids with less than 50 percent EU content that are not covered by an international or reciprocal bilateral agreement. The EU-content requirement applies to U.S suppliers of goods and services in the following sectors: water (production, transport, and distribution of drinking water), energy (gas and heat), urban transport (urban railway, automated systems, tramway, bus, trolley bus, and cable), and postal services.

The Directive's discriminatory provisions were waived for heavy electrical equipment manufactured in the United States under the May 1995 Memorandum of Understanding on Government Procurement between the United States and the EU. In 1993, the United States imposed sanctions on a number of Member States for their implementation of discriminatory provisions of an earlier version of the Directive applicable to telecommunications equipment. Directive 2004/17 clarified that those discriminatory provisions no longer applied to the EU telecommunications sector; the United States thus lifted the sanctions (and the EU lifted reciprocal sanctions against U.S. suppliers) on March 1, 2006.

While U.S. suppliers participate significantly in EU government procurement, the lack of availability of statistics on procurements conducted in EU member states makes it difficult to accurately assess the opportunities available under the GPA to U.S. suppliers.

Other Member State Measures

Member States have their own national practices regarding government procurement. Some Member States require offsets in defense procurement, defined as a contract condition or undertaking that encourages local development or improves a party's balance-of-payments accounts, such as the use of domestic content, the licensing of technology, investment, counter-trade, and similar actions or requirements. Defense procurement related to national security is not covered by the GPA and therefore is not subject to GPA standards. A brief discussion of some of the national practices of particular concern to the United States follows.

Austria

U.S. firms continue to report a strong pro-EU bias and pro-Austrian bias in government contract awards. In major defense purchases related to national security, most government procurement regulations do not apply, and offset requirements can reach up to 200 percent of the value of the contract. Defense offsets in Austria are linked to political considerations and transparency remains limited. Austria's largest military procurement to date, the $2 billion purchase of fighter jets in 2002, was awarded in manner that concerned U.S. defense contractors for its lack of transparency, and apparent bias against a U.S. proposal.

Czech Republic

U.S. and other foreign companies express great concern about the transparency of the public procurement process. Many U.S. bidders report that Czech (or other European) bidders are favored and usually win contract awards despite having less competitive bids and questionable ability to deliver on the terms of the tender. This has been a problem particularly in construction and the purchase of military equipment as well as in the sale of state-owned industries.

Parliament passed a new law on government procurement in 2006, but did little to improve procurement transparency. In fact, the law reduces transparency on construction projects by raising the monetary threshold that would mandate an open public tender from 2 million crowns to 6 million crowns. According to Transparency International, only 27 percent of all public tenders were open to multiple bids in 2005. Bribery in government procurement continues to be a problem. A recent World Bank study noted that the Czech Republic is the only country among the ten EU Members that joined the EU in 2004 where the level of corruption worsened since 2003.

France

France has a strong and extremely competitive aerospace and defense manufacturing base. Having allowed only limited privatization in the sector, the French government continues to maintain shares in several major prime contractors. The French defense market remains difficult but not impossible for non-European competition. Even in the case of European competition, French companies are often selected as prime contractors. Nevertheless, U.S. firms do enjoy success as component and systems suppliers in instances where U.S. products provide capabilities required for interoperability, or where the cost of internal development is prohibitive. The Defense Ministry, which handles around 70 percent of the equipment budget, has a tendency to select non-American contractors, even when their bids cost more and take longer to fulfill the contract. These factors have made it difficult for U.S. defense firms to take part in French/European programs.

Greece

Greece imposes onerous qualification requirements on companies seeking to bid on public procurement tenders. Companies must submit documentation from competent authorities indicating that they have paid taxes, are not in or have not been in bankruptcy, have paid in full their social security obligations for their employees, and other requirements. All board members and the managing director must submit certifications from competent authorities that they have not engaged in fraud, money laundering, criminal activity, or similar activities. These requirements are especially difficult for U.S. firms because there are no competent authorities that issue these types of certifications in the United States. In such cases, companies submitting bids are allowed to submit sworn, notarized, and translated statements from corporate officers. Nonetheless, there exists much confusion among Greek authorities as to how U.S. firms may comply with these requirements.

The government of Greece maintains that it is in the process of reforming and simplifying its procurement laws. According to government officials, new legislation will be released within the next several months.

Greece continues to require offsets as a condition for the awarding of defense contracts.

Ireland

Government procurement in Ireland is generally tendered under open and transparent procurement regulations. U.S. companies have raised concerns, however, that they have been successful in only a few national and regional government tenders, particularly for infrastructure-related procurements. U.S. firms complain that lengthy budgetary decisions delay procurements and that unsuccessful bidders often have difficulty obtaining information on the basis for behind the tender award. Once awarded a contract, companies can experience significant delays in finalizing contracts and commencing work. Successful bidders have also subsequently found that tender documentation does not accurately describe the project conditions under which the procurement is to be conducted.

Italy

Procurement authority is widely dispersed with over 22,000 contracting agencies at the national, regional, and local levels (including regions, municipalities, hospitals, universities, etc.). Italy's public procurement sector is noted for its lack of transparency and corruption, which have created obstacles for some U.S. firms.

Since new laws were implemented in the mid-1990s, corruption has been reduced, but not entirely eliminated, especially at the local level. These laws were enacted after corruption scandals, largely associated with irregularities in public works and public procurement of goods and services, caused an overhaul of procurement personnel.

Lithuania

The public procurement process in Lithuania is not always transparent. Complaints persist that some tenders are so narrowly defined that they appear to be drafted so that only one company can provide the good or service. Since 2003, the government of Lithuania (GOL) has required offset agreements as a condition for the award of contracts for procurement of military equipment exceeding LTL 5 million (about $1.8 million). The GOL purchases most U.S. military equipment using U.S. government grant money, which precludes offsets. The GOL has requested offsets for defense purchases it has made using its own funds. This offset requirement adds an unnecessary level of complexity to exporting military equipment to Lithuania.

Portugal

U.S. firms face stiff competition when bidding against EU firms on procurement projects in Portugal. The Portuguese tend to favor EU firms even when bids from U.S. firms appear technically superior or lower in price. There is a general lack of transparency in procurement procedures. It appears to U.S. firms that they are more successful when investing in joint venture projects with Portuguese or other EU firms.

Slovenia

The Slovenian government has said that it intends to improve the transparency of its public procurement process. The Ministry for Public Administration has also said it will create an e-procurement system, but efforts in this area have stalled. American firms continue to express concerns that the public procurement process in Slovenia is non-transparent. Many American bidders report that European firms are favored and usually win contracts in spite of more costly offers and questionable ability to deliver and service their products. This is a problem across the entire range of public procurement, but it seems most prevalent in telecommunications, medical equipment, and defense procurement.

United Kingdom (UK)

The UK defense market is increasingly defined by the terms of the December 2005 Defence Industrial Strategy (DIS). The document highlights specific sectors and capabilities that the government believes are necessary to retain in the UK; in these areas, procurement will generally be based on partnerships between the Ministry of Defence (MoD) and selected companies. One example is the partnership between the MoD and AgustaWestland for rotorcraft procurement. DIS does not preclude partnerships with non-UK companies and U.S. companies with UK operations could be invited by MoD to form partnerships in key programs in the future. Outside of those areas of partnership highlighted in the DIS, defense procurement is to a large extent an open and competitive process. There have, however, been examples of non-competitive procurements in recent years, as well as instances where a U.S. supplier was initially selected, but the decision was subsequently overturned and the contract awarded to a domestic supplier.

Chapter 6

SUBSIDIES POLICIES

GOVERNMENT SUPPORT FOR AIRBUS

Over many years, the governments of France, Germany, Spain, and the United Kingdom have provided subsidies to their respective Airbus member companies to aid in the development, production and marketing of Airbus large civil aircraft. These governments have financed between 33 and 100 percent of the development costs for all Airbus aircraft models ("launch aid") and provided other forms of support, including equity infusions, debt forgiveness, debt rollovers, and marketing assistance, including political and economic pressure on purchasing governments. The EU's aeronautics research programs are driven significantly by a policy intended to enhance the international competitiveness of the European civil aeronautics industry. EU governments have spent hundreds of millions of euros to create infrastructure needed for Airbus programs, including 751 million euros from the City of Hamburg to purchase land that Airbus is using for the Airbus A380 "superjumbo" project and 182 million euros from French authorities to create the AeroConstellation site, which contains the Airbus facilities for the A380. With more than $6 billion in subsidies, the Airbus A380 is the most heavily subsidized aircraft in history. Some EU governments have also made legally binding commitments of launch aid for the new Airbus A350 aircraft, even though Airbus has not yet repaid any of the financing it received for the A380.

The Airbus Integrated Company – successor to the original Airbus consortium and owned by the European Aeronautic, Defense, and Space Company (EADS) – is now the second-largest aerospace company in the world. With more than half of worldwide deliveries of new large civil aircraft over the last few years, Airbus is a mature company that should face the same commercial risks as its global competitors.

In October 2004, following unsuccessful U.S.-initiated efforts to negotiate a new U.S.-EU agreement that would end subsidies for the development and production of large civil aircraft, the United States submitted a WTO consultation request with respect to the launch aid and other forms of subsidies that EU governments have provided to Airbus. Concurrent with the U.S. WTO consultation request, the United States also exercised its right to terminate the 1992 U.S.–EU bilateral agreement on large civil aircraft. The consultations failed to resolve the U.S. concerns, however, and a renewed effort to negotiate a solution ended without success in April 2005.

Therefore, on May 31, 2005, the United States submitted a WTO panel request. The WTO established the panel on July 20, 2005, and panel proceedings are currently ongoing. U.S. officials have consistently noted their willingness to negotiate a new bilateral agreement on large civil aircraft, even while the WTO litigation proceeds, but have insisted that any such agreement must end launch aid and other direct subsidies for the development and production of such aircraft.

Government Support for Airbus Suppliers

Belgium

The federal government of Belgium, in coordination with Belgium's three regional governments, subsidizes Belgian aircraft component manufacturers that supply parts to the Airbus Integrated Company. Industry sources report about 160 million euros remain from a 195 million federal-regional subsidy package for Airbus A380-related research and development that started in 2001, and that costs covered to date have netted orders worth 1.3 billion euros for the A380. Belgium claims the program was structured in accordance with the 1992 bilateral agreement and covers non-recurring costs. On October 14, 2005, the Belgian federal government made a decision in principle to assist Belgian aviation part producers with 150 million euros of reimbursable public financing, available for nonrecurring development costs for the Airbus A350. Airbus's redesign of the A350 has delayed implementation of this program.

France

In addition to the launch aid that the French government provided for the development of the Airbus A380 super-jumbo aircraft in 2005, France continues to provide reimbursable advances for Airbus programs, engines, helicopters, and on-board equipment. Appropriations in 2006 totaled 218 million euros, of which 168 million euros are committed to the A380. Overall 2006 appropriations, including 55 million euros in support of research and development by industrialists in the sector, amount to 273 million euros.

Spain

The recently completed Puerto Real factory in Spain's Andalucia region is responsible for constructing 10 percent of Airbus' A380 aircraft. Spain's Ministry of Science and Technology currently subsidizes A380 construction through its agreement to provide 376 million euros in direct assistance through 2013.

Furthermore, the regional government of Andalucia has channeled an additional 13 million euros of State General Administration regional incentive funds and 17.5 million euros of its own funds to subsidize the A380 project. Spain has provided numerous additional grants to Airbus' parent company, EADS.

Government Support for Aircraft Engines

United Kingdom (UK)

In February 2001, the UK government announced its intention to provide up to 250 million pounds to Rolls-Royce to support development of two additional engine models for large civil aircraft, the Trent 600 and 900.

The UK government characterized this engine development aid as an "investment" that would provide a "real rate of return" from future sales of the engines.

The European Commission announced its approval of a 250 million pounds "reimbursable advance" without opening a formal investigation into whether the advance constituted an illegal (under EU law) state aid. According to a European Commission statement, the "advance will be reimbursed by Rolls-Royce to the UK government in case of success of the program, based on a levy on engine deliveries and maintenance and support activity." Detailed terms of the approved launch aid were not made public. To date, none of the launch aid for the Trent 600 and 900 has been repaid.

Continuing UK government support of Rolls-Royce raises serious concerns about UK and EU adherence to the WTO Subsidies and Countervailing Measures Agreement. U.S. engine suppliers have lost sales of engines and claim that they have encountered suppressed prices in the United States and world markets.

France

The French government-owned engine manufacturer SNECMA merged with technology and communications firm Sagem to form Safran. The government supports the Safran SaM146 propulsive engine program with a reimbursable advance of 140 million euros.

Canned Fruit Subsidies

The EU continues to subsidize shipments of canned peaches as well as the production of apples, prunes, grapes, wine, cherries, and citrus. Although a 1985 U.S.-EU Canned Fruit Agreement brought some discipline to processing subsidies, significant fraud and abuse have undermined the discipline imposed by the Agreement. Growers and producers of peaches receive a range of assistance from producer aid, market withdrawal subsidies, sugar export rebates, producer organization aid, and regional development assistance. The United States will continue to monitor EU subsidies to this sector and evaluate their trade-distorting effects.

Wood Industry Subsidies

Several EU Member States and regional governments within them provided state aid to pulp, paper, and wood processing projects. Germany, in particular, has given aid in the form of grants, loans, and loan guarantees for pulp and paper and wood processing operations, especially in eastern Germany. These subsidy programs are part of the overall combined EU/national regional support programs. This has added substantial new capacity and has contributed to a substantial drop in U.S. pulp and paper exports to the EU and world markets, while fostering a rise in European paper and lumber and wooden panel exports to the United States and third country markets. A combination of factors, namely robust growth in the construction sector and duties put on Canadian softwood lumber, has also increased the competitiveness of German construction lumber in the United States.

Chapter 7

Intellectual Property Rights (IPR) Protection

Overview

The EU and its Member States support strong protection for intellectual property rights (IPR). Together, the U.S. and the EU have committed to enforcing IPR in third countries and at our borders in the EU-U.S. Action Strategy endorsed at the June 2006 U.S.-EU Summit. In 2006, the European Commission issued communications on strengthening the criminal law framework to combat intellectual property offenses, and a renewed effort to introduce a community patent.

The United States has raised concerns regarding the IPR practices of the EU or its Member States, either through the U.S. Special 301 process or through WTO Dispute Settlement procedures concerning failure to fully implement the WTO Agreement on Trade-Related Aspects of Intellectual Property Rights (TRIPS). The United States continues to be engaged with the EU and individual Member States on these matters.

In April 2004, the EU adopted a Directive on the enforcement of intellectual and industrial property rights, such as copyright and related rights, trademarks, designs, and patents. This Directive requires all Member States to apply effective and proportionate remedies and penalties that form a deterrent against those engaged in counterfeiting and piracy. Member States are required to have a similar set of measures, procedures, and remedies available for rights holders to defend their IPR. Member States were supposed to have implemented the Directive by April 2006. At present, only about one half of the Member States have transposed the legislation.

Designs

The EU adopted a Regulation introducing a single Community system for the protection of designs in December 2001. The Regulation provides for two types of design protection, directly applicable in each EU Member State: the registered Community design and the unregistered Community design. Under the registered Community design system, holders of eligible designs can use an inexpensive procedure to register designs with the EU's Office for Harmonization in the Internal Market (OHIM). The holders will then be granted exclusive rights to use the designs anywhere in the EU for up to 25 years. Unregistered Community designs that meet the Regulation's requirements are automatically protected for three years from the date of disclosure of the design to the public. Protection for any registered Community design was automatically extended to the ten new EU Member States on May 1, 2004.

The European Commission has proposed amending the Legal Protection of Designs Directive (98/71) by removing Member States' option to maintain design protection for "visible" replacement vehicle parts, such as hoods, bumpers, doors, lamps, rear protection panels, windscreens, and wings. The proposal would allow independent part manufacturers, not linked to the producers of finished vehicles, to compete throughout the EU market for visible replacement parts. Neither non-visible parts, like engine or mechanical parts, nor components in new vehicles would be affected by the proposal.

Patents

Patent filing and maintenance fees in the EU and its Member States are significantly higher than in other countries. Fees associated with the filing, issuance, and maintenance of a patent over its life far exceed those in the United States.

In some countries, such as Portugal, copies of medicines that are still under patent are allowed on the market by the Ministries of Health.

Data Exclusivity

In some of the new Member States in particular, there is a lack of protection for data submitted to obtain marketing approval for pharmaceutical and agricultural chemical products. Article 39.3 of the Trade-Related Aspects of Intellectual Property Rights (TRIPS) Agreement requires such protection.

Bulgaria

The U.S. pharmaceutical industry is concerned about Bulgarian legislation that requires a valid patent as a prerequisite for obtaining data protection. Bulgaria is reportedly considering legislation to eliminate this requirement.

Hungary

Hungary's 2001 ministerial decree on the protection of test data took effect on January 1, 2003. Retroactive protection exists for pharmaceutical products that received first marketing authorization in the EU or Hungary on or after April 12, 2001. However, Hungary generally does not provide an effective system to prevent the issuance of marketing approvals for unauthorized patent-infringing copies of pharmaceutical products, and patent infringements are dealt with by administrative courts lacking expert knowledge, or the power to take injunctive measures.

Poland

Concerns remain over delays in full implementation of the EU data protection regime. Polish law currently supports the EU data protection regime for drugs centrally registered at the EU level. For drugs nationally registered in Poland, however, (in practice, those drugs registered before Poland's EU accession) Polish law provides for only 6 years of data exclusivity. Poland requested that the European Commission delay implementation of the EU requirement for 15 years. The Commission has not informed Poland of its final decision. In addition, while the government has signaled that it is considering implementation of a coordination mechanism between the Health Ministry and the patent agency, no concrete actions have been taken to do so.

Portugal

In September 2006, Portugal enacted the Consumption of Medicine in Hospitals statute, an adaptation of EU Directive 2004/27/EC. The statute extends data exclusivity from six years to ten and only requires companies to renew licenses once after five years as opposed to every five years. However, the statute also states that the Ministry of Health does not need to cross-check with the Ministry of Economy for existing patents before granting licenses to generic drug manufacturers. According to industry sources, this latter aspect of the legislation may cost U.S. pharmaceutical companies over $500,000 in lost sales and tens of thousands more in legal fees.

PATENTING OF BIOTECHNOLOGICAL INVENTIONS

A 1998 EU Directive (98/44) on the legal protection of biotechnological inventions harmonizes EU Member State rules on patent protection for biotechnological inventions. Although Member States were required to bring their national laws into compliance with the Directive by July 2000, some had not yet fully met that obligation, and the European Commission has started legal proceedings at the European Court of Justice against them.

TRADEMARKS

Registration of trademarks with the European Union's Office for Harmonization in the Internal Market (OHIM) began in 1996. OHIM issues a single Community trademark that is valid in all EU Member States.

MADRID PROTOCOL

On October 1, 2004, the European Community acceded to the World Intellectual Property Organization (WIPO) Madrid Protocol, establishing a link between the Madrid Protocol system, administered by WIPO, and the Community Trademark system, administered by OHIM. Community Trademark applicants and holders now are allowed to apply for international protection of their trademarks through the filing of an international application under the Madrid Protocol.

Conversely, holders of international registrations under the Madrid Protocol will be entitled to apply for protection of their trademarks under the Community Trademark system.

GEOGRAPHICAL INDICATIONS (GI)

The United States has long had concerns that the EU's system for the protection of geographical indications, reflected in Community Regulation 1493/99 for wines and spirits and in previous Regulation 2081/92 for certain other agricultural products and foodstuffs, appears to fall short of what is required under the TRIPS Agreement.

As a result of a WTO dispute launched by the United States, the WTO Dispite Settlement Body ruled on April 20, 2005, that the EC's regulation on food-related geographical indications (GIs) was inconsistent with the EC's obligations under the TRIPS Agreement and the GATT 1994. In its report, the DSB agreed that the EC's GI regulation impermissibly discriminated against non-EC products and persons, and agreed with the United States that the regulation could not create broad exceptions to trademark rights guaranteed by the TRIPS Agreement. In response, the EC published an amended GI regulation in April 2006 that is intended to implement the DSB's recommendations and rulings. The United States continues to have some concerns about this amended regulation and is carefully monitoring its application.

ADDITIONAL MEMBER STATE PRACTICES

Belgium

While Belgium transposed the EU Copyright Directive into national law in May 2005, it failed to meet the April 2006 deadline to implement the Enforcement Directive. Belgium also has not implemented EU Regulation 1383/2003 concerning customs actions against goods suspected of infringing certain intellectual property rights. Domestically pirated and parallel-imported DVDs are a growing problem in Belgium. An industry trade association estimates that 250,000 illegal downloads of DVDs occur daily in Belgium, and illegal copies on

VHS, CD-R and DVD-R media are distributed by specialty stores, retail outlets, and local and international Internet sites. The recording industry estimates that 85 percent of blank digital media sold in Belgium are used for illegal downloads of music or videos. Annual losses to the U.S. motion picture industry through IPR piracy in Belgium are estimated at over 15 million euros. Belgium's 1994 Copyright Law provides deterrent penalties for piracy, but legal procedures are cumbersome and the court system is overburdened. Obtaining a judicial restraining order against Internet piracy, for example, takes two to three months, and judges demand proof of damages to assign more than token fines. However, the country's first-ever prison sentence for copyright piracy was imposed in April 2006, and Belgium was the first of the EU-15 to ratify the WIPO Copyright Treaty in May 2006.

Bulgaria

Overall optical disc piracy has dropped, but largely due to an increase in piracy over the Internet. While the government has taken a number of significant steps to combat piracy, these actions have not yet led to significant convictions, and the piracy rate has not fallen drastically. Furthermore, Bulgaria is still widely used for the transshipment of pirated compact discs from Russia and Ukraine to the Balkans, Greece, and Turkey. Bulgarian legislation was further amended to harmonize with EU requirements and to provide a better legal framework for efficient IPR enforcement. The laws that were amended include the Law on Copyright and Related Rights, the Law on Patents, the Law on Marks and Geographical Indications, the Law on Industrial Design and Art, 172a (copyright and related rights criminal offences) and 172b (industrial property rights criminal offences) of the Penal Code of the Republic of Bulgaria. In September 2005, the parliament approved the long awaited Law on Administrative Control over the Manufacture and Distribution of Optical Disc Media, which now requires source identification code on blank optical discs produced in Bulgaria and strengthens the import/export regime for raw materials and equipment involved in optical disk production.

Cyprus

IPR legislation in Cyprus is, on the whole, modern and comprehensive, although enforcement should be further improved. Cyprus has harmonized its IPR regime with EU requirements as part of its accession to the EU in 2004. According to industry sources, the level of DVD and CD piracy continues at roughly 50 percent. Software piracy, largely fueled by small personal computer assembly and sale operations, has declined to 53 percent but is still significantly above the European average. Internet piracy is a growing concern.

Czech Republic

Although the Czech Republic has made progress in strengthening anti-piracy legislation and enforcement, significant problems remain with piracy and counterfeiting in open-air markets near the Czech border. New amendments were added in 2006 to the Copyright Law and the Law on Consumer Protection, which grants the Customs Office, a law enforcement agency with over 6,000 armed inspectors, greater authority to seize counterfeit products and requires all marketplace sellers to register with the municipality. The level of IPR piracy is rising and several IPR watchdog groups, especially from the recording and manufacturing industries, have recommended the Czech Republic be placed on the Special 301 Priority Watch List. There are also problems in court proceedings. Court cases, including IPR related cases, can often stretch to five years on average, and even then the current system for the calculation and collection of damages favor defendants according to legal experts who work in the field.

France

Although the French government has significantly stepped up its efforts to fight piracy, video piracy and unauthorized parallel imports continue to impose losses on U.S. industry, and cable piracy and Internet piracy continue to present further problems in this area. France was the last Member State to pass legislation implementing the EU Copyright Directive in August 2006. Some U.S. stakeholders have expressed concerns with the provisions of that law related to digital rights management and technological protection measures, which may result in the forced disclosure and use of technical information that may be protected by intellectual property such as copyright, patents and trade secrets.

Germany

Non-retail outlets (Internet, print media, mail order, open-air markets) are the primary distribution channels for pirated goods in Germany. Pirated videos, VCDs, and DVDs are sold primarily by residential mail-order dealers who offer the products via the Internet or through newspaper advertisements, or directly sell them in flea markets. German copyright legislation allows the making of private copies, which, although it does not include sharing or downloading of music, has been sometimes misunderstood as being a broad exception. Starting in 2005, the German entertainment industry has blanketed the country with commercials as an information campaign to educate the public regarding the problem of piracy, especially on the Internet. While German federal authorities have been receptive to

U.S. IPR concerns, there have been mixed results at the German state-level, which can have broad impact due to Germany's decentralized law enforcement structure. German authorities in several cases have prosecuted pirates who downloaded music and videos from the Internet and then distributed burned CDs or DVDs. In October 2004, they arrested four individuals who ran a major ring selling pirated videos on the Internet. The German government in July 2003 enacted amendments to the German Copyright Act intended to bring it in line with the EU Copyright/"Information Society" Directive. The Ministry of Justice has introduced additional amendments to the copyright law that are likely to be considered by Parliament in 2007. U.S. publishers have expressed a concern that these amendments might result in insufficient protections for copyrighted works, particularly those in digital format. The United States continues to engage the German government on the issue.

Greece

Although protection of intellectual property rights in Greece is better than it was during the last decade, there are troubling signs that violations, particularly in copyrighted audio-visual products and apparel and footwear, are once again on the rise. Despite the existence of adequate IPR legislation, a major problem appears to be a reluctance on the part of Greek judges to sentence IPR violators to jail, or impose fines of a high enough level to act as a deterrent. The United States welcomes initiatives by the government of Greece to make efforts to educate the judiciary on IPR matters to discourage this trend.

Hungary

Hungary acceded to the European Patent Convention on January 1, 2003 and has amended the Hungarian Patent Act accordingly. Act CII of 2003 modified the Hungarian Copyright Act and the Hungarian Design Act in order to bring them in line with the relevant EU legislation. The Hungarian Patent Office implemented the EU Copyright/"Information Society" Directive. In October 2004, Hungary implemented Council Regulation 1383/2003, concerning customs action against goods suspected of infringing certain intellectual property rights. Further, a government decree established a customs task force to accept claims from producers whose trademarks or copyrights were infringed.

Italy

Italy's anti-piracy laws, which also address Internet piracy, are among the toughest in Europe. However, Italy possesses one of the highest overall piracy rates in Western Europe due to a lack of adequate enforcement efforts. Italian judges rarely hand down meaningful jail sentences for cases of IPR theft, and are seen as the weak link in Italy's efforts to combat piracy effectively. Leaders in industry, government and academia all say a change in public perception of the seriousness of IPR crimes is needed before there can be better IPR protection in Italy.

In April 2005, the Italian government created a "High Commissioner" position to coordinate IPR protection. Seizures of counterfeit and pirated goods by Italian authorities increased in the past year, though enforcement varies widely from region to region. Italian law allows police to impose a fine of up to 10,000 euros for possession of fake goods. While this tough measure increased public awareness of IPR crime, there is only sporadic enforcement. Street vendors continue to openly sell pirated and counterfeited goods.

Lithuania

Estimates of piracy levels of optical media, software, and motion pictures in Lithuania vary, but it remains a problem. The situation appears to be improving, however. Lithuania adopted legislation in 2006 that harmonizes Lithuania's laws with EU regulations, strengthening IPR protection by increasing penalties and making it easier for prosecutors to present necessary evidence. The Lithuanian government has demonstrated the political will to enforce IPR protections in specific cases, but the government needs to continue to improve its efficacy in combating piracy. The Lithuanian government made progress in early 2007 by closing down a notorious Internet pirate website, but should continue enforcement efforts agains Internet piracy.

Poland

Poland has shown progress on several elements of IP protection. The Polish government has increased anti-piracy efforts, improving enforcement at the Warsaw Stadium and in the border bazaars frequented by German tourists and others. In addition, the Interministerial Antipiracy Group published an IPR strategy that emphasizes cooperation with industry. Although Poland has made some progress in strengthening border enforcement in conjunction with rights-holders, problems remain both along the eastern and western borders with importation and sale of counterfeit alcohol, tobacco, and pirate optical discs. As border enforcement continues to strengthen, Internet piracy of movies and music is also becoming a more serious problem. According to an anti-piracy group, the Polish court system is currently overburdened with nearly five thousand pending IPR protection cases, many of which are not scheduled to be prosecuted for several years.

Romania

Although authorities have made gradual improvements, the rates of copyright piracy are high in Romania. Levels of DVD piracy have risen to 80 percent, while levels of videocassette piracy are down to 20 percent and the most blatant retail piracy has been eliminated. While product was mainly smuggled into the market in the past, concerns are rising that capacity to produce in Romania may be growing. Another area of concern is the illegal sale of counterfeit decoder devices and stealing video signals from cable services. The appointment in 2003 of a special IPR prosecutor in the General Prosecutor's Office (GPO) and the establishment of a small IPR office in the GPO in 2005 have improved enforcement, but few IPR cases are prosecuted.

Spain

Copyright infringement remains a serious problem with illegal Internet downloads becoming increasingly important. Content provider companies say that Internet Service Providers resist their requests to move aggressively against websites illegally trafficking in copyrighted material and in shutting down service to illegal downloaders. There is a government-organized working group on Internet governance including both sets of stakeholders but so far no solution has been found.

Sweden

Sweden remains a major contributor to the worldwide problem of Internet piracy. Although the police raid against Pirate Bay (the world's largest Bit Torrent tracker) sent shockwaves through international file-sharing circles, the fact that Pirate Bay was back in operation within a few days casts a shadow over the forceful actions of the Swedish authorities and prospective legal action against the operators is likely to take time. Sweden is also still a host to a large part of the world's "top sites" for piracy and the largest number of DC++ file-sharing hubs and users.

The legislative and enforcement framework in Sweden is generally effective against conventional hard goods piracy but actual enforcement with respect to Internet piracy has been weak. In the last year, however, the Swedish government has repeatedly signaled to police and prosecutors that it wants to step up efforts to curb Internet piracy. The government has also requested that the industry provide legal alternatives to file-sharing, and it has appointed a government commission to look into possibilities to encourage such a development.

In the last year, several cases of illegal distribution of copyrighted material on the Internet have been tried in the Swedish courts. The courts have successfully used existing legislation to sentence defendants for the infringing activities. The Swedish government also is working on strengthening existing laws to make it easier for law enforcement officials to meet evidentiary requirements.

Chapter 8

SERVICES BARRIERS

CONCERNS RELATED TO EU ENLARGEMENT

On May 28, 2004, the European Commission notified members of the World Trade Organization of a proposed consolidation of the EU's schedule of specific commitments under the General Agreement on Trade in Services (GATS) pursuant to GATS Article V to reflect both the 1995 accession to the European Union of Austria, Finland, and Sweden, and the 2004 accession of Cyprus, the Czech Republic, Estonia, Hungary, Latvia, Lithuania, Malta, Poland, the Slovak Republic, and Slovenia. As a result of this proposed consolidation, a number of previous GATS commitments by these countries have been modified in a way that may reduce sector-specific or horizontal market access commitments. Although not within the scope of the EU's GATS Article V notification, the EU's consolidation proposal also entails the extension to the new Member States of most-favored nation exemptions reflected in the EU's existing schedule of GATS commitments.

Following GATS rules, which allow a Member to reduce or withdraw commitments provided that they negotiate offsetting compensation to maintain the overall level of market access, the United States closely worked with Brazil, Hong Kong, Japan, Canada and 12 other WTO Members to negotiate a compensation package with the European Union. Negotiations were successfully completed on September 25, 2006. The agreed compensation package contains new and enhanced commitments in several other services sectors, including public utilities, engineering, computer, advertising, and financial services.

Television Broadcast Directive (Television without Frontiers Directive)

The 1989 EU Broadcast Directive (also known as the Television without Frontiers Directive) includes a provision requiring that a majority of television transmission time be reserved for European-origin programs "where practicable and by appropriate means." All EU Member States, including the Member States that acceded to the EU in May 2004 and January 2007, have enacted legislation to implement the Broadcast Directive. It remains important to ensure that the flexibility built into the Directive is preserved and that individual broadcasting markets are allowed to develop according to their specific conditions and needs.

In December, 2005, the European Commission adopted a proposal for revising the Television without Frontiers Directive. The proposal distinguishes between "linear" services (scheduled broadcasting via traditional TV or other means which "pushes" content) and "non-linear" services (such as on-demand films or other news which the viewer "pulls" from a network). TV broadcasting rules would apply to linear services in a modernized, more flexible form, while non-linear services (which are not covered under the 1989 directive) would be subject to a set of basic principles, including the protection of minors and prevention of incitement to racial hatred. The proposal maintains the country of origin principle. The Culture Committee of the European Parliament issued a report on the proposal in August, 2006. The legislation, which requires approval of the European Parliament and Member States, is not expected to be finalized until late 2007 or possibly 2008.

Several EU Member States have specific legislation that hinders the free flow of some programming. A summary of some of the more salient restrictive national practices follows.

France

France continues to apply its more restrictive version of the EU Broadcast Directive which was first introduced into French legislation and approved by the European Commission in 1992. In implementing the Directive, France chose to specify a percentage of European programming (60 percent) and French programming (40 percent) which exceeded the requirements of the Broadcast Directive. Moreover, these quotas apply to both the 24-hour day and prime time slots, and the definition of prime time differs from network to network. The prime time rules are a significant barrier to access of U.S. programs to the French market. In addition, the United States continues to be concerned that radio broadcast quotas which have been in effect since 1996 (40 percent of songs on almost all French private and public radio stations must be Francophone), limit broadcasts of American music.

Italy

Legislation passed in 1998 that made Italy's TV broadcast quota stricter than the EU Broadcast Directive remains in effect. The legislation makes 51 percent European content mandatory during prime time, and excludes talk shows from the programming that may be counted toward fulfilling the quota. A 1998 regulation also requires all multiplex movie theaters of more than 1,300 seats to reserve 15 to 20 percent of their seats, distributed over no fewer than three screens, to showing EU films. In May 2004, Italy enacted controversial media reform through the "Gasparri Law," under which the media/communications market is considered one sector. Under this law, no single operator may receive more than 20 percent of the sector's total revenues. In addition, the law provides for the gradual privatization of RAI, the state-owned radio and television broadcasting conglomerate. The government of Italy is in the process of reconsidering Gasparri Law provisions.

Spain

Spain's theatrical film system has been modified sufficiently in recent years so that it is no longer a major source of trade friction. Government regulations issued in 1997 require exhibitors to show one day of EU-produced film for every three days of non-EU-produced film. Spanish law requires that the quotas issue be reviewed in 2006. The Ministry of Culture is currently preparing a draft Film Law.

POSTAL SERVICES

United States service and package service providers have in the past expressed concern that postal monopolies in many EU Member States restrict their market access and create unfair conditions of competition with the incumbents.

With the adoption of the Postal Services Directive, the European Union in 1997 took a first step to get national postal monopolies to gradually open up to competition. A second Directive in 2002 succeeded in opening up a number of postal services -- including all outgoing cross-border mail -- but stopped short of liberalizing the market for the delivery of letters weighing less than 50 grams. On October 18, 2006, the European Commission adopted a proposal to open up postal markets to full, unrestricted competition by 2009. The proposal is subject to approval by the Member States and the European Parliament and is expected to go into effect in summer 2007.

Belgium

While the Belgian Post has taken measures in recent years to liberalize, industry competitors continue to express concerns about market access and a postal monopoly operating in Belgium. January 2006 legislation introduced a licensing regime for universal postal services as well as a compensation fund for universal service. The licensing regime would provide revenue to the Belgian Post if liberalization proved unprofitable due to its universal service obligation. Under the current legal framework, express companies appear to be exempt from the licensing regime as well as from the obligation to provide for a compensation fund for universal service on the condition that these services are clearly distinct from the universal postal service by virtue of their value-added characteristics.

Germany

In February 2005, the Federal Regulatory Agency (Bundesnetzagentur) took action against Deutsche Post AG (DPAG), in response to complaints from competitors. Its ruling forbids DPAG from hindering or discriminating against rival small- and medium-sized providers of mail preparation services, especially those collecting and presorting letters and feeding mail items weighing less than 100 grams into DPAG's sorting centers. This ruling follows an October 2004 move by the European Commission to initiate a treaty infringement procedure against Germany for failing to mandate that DPAG offer unbundled access to competitors. Some U.S. companies have indicated they might be interested in providing services such as sorting.

Ireland

Currently, postal services "reserved" to An Post, the national postal agency and Ireland's designated Universal Service Provider, are confined to items of domestic correspondence and incoming cross-border correspondence weighing 50g or less. All mail falling outside this category is open to competition and can be handled by any mail/package company operating in the Irish market. From January 2009, the postal market will be fully open to competition and other operators will be free to handle any mail now reserved to An Post.

PROFESSIONAL SERVICES

In the area of professional services, there are significant variations among EU Member State requirements for foreign lawyers and accountants intending to practice in the European Union. While many of these are not outright barriers, disparities among Member State requirements can complicate access to the European market for U.S. lawyers and accountants.

LEGAL SERVICES

Austria

U.S. citizens can only provide legal advice on U.S. law and public international law (excluding EU law) on a temporary basis. Only an Austrian or other EU national can join the Bar Association. U.S. nationals cannot represent clients before Austrian courts and authorities, and cannot establish a commercial presence in Austria. However, informal cooperation with Austrian partners is possible.

Czech Republic

The Czech Republic requires that all attorneys be members of the Czech bar. U.S. educated lawyers may register with the Czech Bar and take an equivalency exam, but are limited to practicing home state (U.S.) law and international law. To represent clients in Czech courts, U.S. lawyers must first undergo a three-year legal traineeship and pass the Czech bar exam. U.S. firms are allowed to cooperate with local firms and lend them their name; as a result, firms that operate in the country do so as independent Czech branches. They may have U.S. attorneys that are attached to the staffs as "advisors."

Finland

Foreigners from non-EU countries cannot become members of the Finnish Bar Association and receive the higher law profession title of Asianajaja (Attorney at Law). Persons holding the title of Asianajaja are subject to Asianajaja Law as well as bar regulations. While the title gives added prestige and helps solicit clients, it is not essential to practice domestic or international law or to represent a client in court.

France

Non-EU firms are not permitted to establish branch offices in France under their own names. Also, non-EU lawyers and firms are not permitted to form partnerships with or hire French lawyers.

Germany

U.S. lawyers that have joined the German Bar Association under their home title may practice international law (but not EU law) and the law of their home country. To be admitted to the bar to practice German law, individuals generally have to complete five years of study, then successfully complete the first of two state exams. After successfully completing the first exam they undertake two years of practical training. Individuals then take the second state exam, and upon passing, are admitted to the bar.

Hungary

Foreign non-EU lawyers may provide legal advice on legislation of their own country and international law. Lawyers registered in the EU may be admitted to the bar. Foreign lawyers from non-EU countries may establish a partnership with a Hungarian legal firm and provide legal services under a "cooperation agreement."

Ireland

In general, lawyers with non-Irish qualifications who wish to practice Irish law and appear before Irish courts must either pass transfer examinations or retrain as lawyers under the direction of the Law Society of Ireland. Only lawyers who have either been admitted to the Bar of England, Wales, or Northern Ireland, practiced as an attorney in New York, California, Pennsylvania (with five years experience required in Pennsylvania), or New Zealand, or have been admitted as lawyers in either an EU or EFTA Member State are entitled to take the transfer examination.

Italy

In 2001, Italy passed a law implementing EU Directive 98/5 on EU lawyers' freedom to establish themselves EU-wide and enabling Italian lawyers to practice jointly, including with EU lawyers, through a limited liability partnership or through the Italian branch of a partnership formed in another EU Member State, as long as the limited liability partnership is composed exclusively of Italian and EU lawyers. The status of non-EU lawyers is not explicitly addressed by the law. This omission leaves the status of international law firms with offices in Italy uncertain, insofar as they have Italian and non-EU lawyers as partners. Despite this ambiguity, several major U.S. law firms have a presence in Italy.

Lithuania

Only EU citizens may join the Lithuanian bar and establish law firms that provide the full range of legal services. Lithuanian law permits U.S. attorneys to establish law offices that provide paralegal services. These firms differ from traditional law firms, however, in that they cannot compel Lithuanian institutions to provide information, nor can they protect legally the lawyer-client privilege.

U.S. firms can, however, easily partner with a local law firm to provide a full range of legal services.

Slovakia

In August 2006, the Slovak Antimonopoly Office overturned Act No. 586/2003 (the Advocacy Act) which was designed to force non-EU-based law firms to change their legal status from a branch partnership to a limited liability company (LLC). Under the Advocacy Act, an LLC had to be owned by an EU advocate registered in Slovakia or a Slovak national, and non-EU law firms could not market themselves under their internationally recognized corporate identities, incurring extra costs to comply with the special rules. The ruling also overturned the Slovak Bar's internal rules that restrict a firm's name to that of living partners. The Slovak Antimonopoly Office found that the rules contravened Article 81 of the Founding Treaty of the European Community, as well as Slovakia's own Act on the Protection of Economic Competition.

The Slovak law still requires non-EU-based lawyers and law firms to register with the Slovak Bar Association to practice law in Slovakia. In 2006, no U.S. attorneys have been able to register. The United States is concerned that the Slovak Bar consistently has tried to limit foreign lawyers' ability to practice law in Slovakia; this provision of the Advocacy Act appears to facilitate its ability to deny foreign lawyers registration.

ACCOUNTING AND AUDITING SERVICES

France

There is a nationality requirement for the establishment of a practice, which can be waived at the discretion of the French authorities. An applicant for such a permit, however, must have lived in France for at least five years.

Greece

U.S. access to the Greek accounting market remains limited. A 1997 Presidential decree established a method for fixing minimum fees for audits and established restrictions on the use of different types of personnel in audits. It also prohibited auditing firms from doing multiple tasks for a client, thus raising the cost of audit work. The Greek government has defended these regulations as necessary to ensure the quality and objectivity of audits.

Hungary

Only Hungarian-certified accountants may conduct audits, but this individual may work for a foreign-owned firm.

ARCHITECTURAL SERVICES

The U.S. National Council for Architectural Registration Boards and the EU Architect's Council of Europe signed a joint recommendation for a Mutual Recognition Agreement for Architects in November 2005. The U.S. Government and the European Commission will collaborate with relevant regulators and professional associations to consider options for the promotion of progress towards such an agreement in accordance with each side's legal systems.

Austria

Only citizens from EU and EEA Member States are eligible to obtain a license to provide independent architectural services in Austria. This restriction does not appear to be reflected in the European Communities' Schedule of Specific Commitments under the GATS.

FINANCIAL SERVICES

Poland

Citibank and other service providers have requested that the Polish government treat independent legal persons as a single taxable person as allowed by the EU VAT Directive. VAT grouping is already employed by the UK, the Netherlands, Ireland, Germany, Austria, Denmark, Finland and Sweden. VAT grouping would allow financial service providers to recover VAT charges they incur upon making intra-company payments for supplies, including labor costs.

TELECOMMUNICATIONS MARKET ACCESS

Both the WTO commitments covering telecommunications services and the EU's Common Regulatory Framework for Electronic Communications Networks and Services (Framework Directive), have encouraged liberalization and competition in the European telecommunications sector. As part of the WTO Agreement, for example, all EU Member States made commitments to provide market access and national treatment for voice telephony and data services. The Framework Directive imposes additional liberalization and harmonization requirements, and the Commission has taken action against Member States that have not implemented the Framework Directive. However, implementation of these requirements has been uneven across Member States and in many markets significant problems remain, including with the provisioning and pricing of unbundled local loops, line sharing, co-location, and the provisioning of leased lines. Partial government ownership of some Member States' incumbent telecommunications operators also has the potential to raise problems for new entrants.

In 2002, the EU issued a new regulatory framework for electronic communications that includes the EU Framework Directive and four specific Directives on: (1) licensing; (2) access and interconnection; (3) universal service and user rights; and (4) data protection.

This new regulatory framework requires Member States to update and adapt legislation to account for converging technologies and for future technological and market developments. It applies to all forms of electronic communications networks and associated services, not just traditional fixed telephony networks. The long-term goal is to phase out sector-specific, *ex-ante* regulation (for all but public interest reasons) in favor of reliance on general competition rules.

Beginning in December 2005, the European Commission began a process of reviewing the directives under the regulatory framework for electronic communications, and the European Commission is expected to make proposals for revising the directives in mid-2007.

Member State Practices

Enforcement of existing legislation by the National Regulating Authorities (NRAs) has been hampered by unnecessarily lengthy and cumbersome procedures in France, Italy, Austria, and Portugal, among others. The European Commission has also found that incumbents in Germany, Greece, Spain, Italy, Ireland, Austria,

Finland, and Sweden have slowed the arrival of competition by systematically appealing their national regulators' decisions.

Austria

In general, Austria has moved toward a more open and competitive telecommunications market and has implemented the relevant directives. There are several outstanding concerns related to: (1) the unbundling of the "last mile," (2) deficient procedures for the wholesale broadband access market (including bitstream access), (3) problems with the wholesale line rental, (4) interconnection fees and (5) the market for public telecommunications transit services. Generally, Austria's NRA – the TKC – provides timely initial decisions, but follow-up on those decisions, including the appeals process for such decisions, remains uncertain and slow.

Finland

Finland has one of the most mature mobile markets in Europe, with overall penetration rates in 2006 above the EU average. Fierce competition and a tough regulatory environment have created a difficult market for mobile operators. Finland has the third lowest mobile call charges of all Member States, behind only Denmark and Luxemburg. The merger of Telia and Sonera in 2002 reduced the number of competitors, since Telia in consequence relinquished its Finnish mobile business, and in late 2005 Tele2 also withdrew.

Finnish mobile phone operators have slowed the arrival of competition by systematically appealing the Finnish NRA – Finnish Communications Regulatory Authority FICORA's SMP (significant market power) decisions. The appeal processes have played an important role in the effectiveness of regulation in Finland, and appeals can take several years. Recent cases from Finland, where appeals have taken as long as three to five years, underscore the fact that the current system creates a high degree of regulatory uncertainty.

France

French cell phone usage is finally catching up to the European average, topping 80 percent penetration in 2006.

France implemented the EU Framework Directive in 2004, and the NRA (ARCEP) has made some progress in subsequently conducting the required market analyses of telecommunications sectors.

France Telecom (FT) was fined 80 million euros in July 2006 by a French Court of Appeals, which had found the company abused its position as France's dominant telecommunications operator by blocking access for rival ADSL Internet operators to its network between 1999 and 2002. The appeals court upheld an earlier decision by the French Competition Council, which has been playing an increasingly important role in the telecommunications sector as France Telecom struggles to maintain its dominant position. FT's domination is no longer a given as innovative technologies are deployed to offer "triple play" (long distance, Internet, and television) and even "four play" (triple play plus mobile telephone) packages at cut rate prices.

Germany

Germany has made slow progress in introducing competition to some sectors of its telecommunications market. The revised Telecommunications Act entered into force in June 2004 and most competitors to DT believe that it should facilitate enhanced competition. New entrants report they continue to face difficulties competing with the partially state-owned incumbent Deutsche Telekom AG (DT), which retains a near-monopoly in a number of key services, including local loop and broadband connections. On the positive side, greater competition for local and long-distance calling has helped competitors gain more than 20 percent of the local calling market since 2003. Currently, the National Regulatory Agency is studying how it should regulate 18 individual market segments, as required by the Framework Directive. After more than a year, it has completed twelve market studies.

In 2006, the German government amended the Telecommunications Act to boost customer protection rules, including more transparent pricing and billing, and introduce liability limitations for service providers. Section 9a of the amended Act, which took effect in February 2007, may grant "regulatory holidays" for services in new markets. DT has lobbied hard for such an exemption; competitors complain that Section 9a will shield DT from regulation as it installs a lucrative fiber optic network in order to provide triple play services. Since DT lacks a significant competitor capable of making a similar offering, this provision risks creating a *de facto* monopoly for services which do not meet the criteria of a "new market." The U.S. Government has raised serious concerns and engaged the

German government repeatedly on this issue. The European Commissioner for Information Society initiated infringement proceedings immediately after Section 9a entered into force.

Companies have complained that DT and other mobile providers charge excessive termination rates when fixed-line users call mobile phones. After a June 2004 voluntary agreement by mobile operators failed to reduce termination charges and under continued EU pressure, the Federal Network Agency directed mobile providers in August 2006 to lower termination charges to a cost-based level. In addition, in October 2005, in response to complaints by competitors, the National Regulatory Agency launched a probe into whether DT is violating its dominant market position with the offer of a new low-cost ISDN Internet connection subscription fee. In September 2006, it issued a ruling requiring DT to grant competitors, upon request, IP bitstream access to residential customers, such as unbundled broadband access based on the Internet protocol.

Hungary

The Hungarian telecommunications market is almost fully liberalized. However, legal obstacles, as well as a lack of investors, have hindered competition. In May 2005, following the general policy of majority owner Deutsche Telekom (DT), the Hungarian "T-Brands" (Axelero, the Internet service provider; the business solutions branch; and the cable provider branch) merged with Matáv, the former monopolist and today's market-leading telephony provider, under the name of Magyar Telekom Rt. In October 2005, Magyar Telekom Rt. merged with T-Mobile Hungary, the leading mobile phone operator, which is also partially owned by DT. This involved changes in management and strengthened Magyar Telekom's leading position in the voice and communications market. UPC and TELE2, as new-fixed line providers, launched their services offering lower tariffs than Matav. In addition, UPC has focused on bundling television, broadband Internet and telephony services to gain larger market share in an ever-shrinking fixed-line telephony environment. The number of fixed line subscriptions decreased to 33.8 percent by the end of the second quarter of 2006, while mobile phone penetration continues to increase, reaching nearly 94 percent at the end of the same quarter.

Ireland

The government privatized the state monopoly, Telecom Eireann, in 1999, and the new company, Eircom, retains a 74 percent share of the fixed lines in Ireland and dominates leased-line services and national interconnection, entailing high prices for local services. Competition in the Irish communications market intensified in 2006, with an ever-growing number of authorised operators. There were also several high-profile mergers and acquisitions, notably the purchase of a majority stake in Eircom by Australia-based Babcock and Brown in June 2006. There are four mobile operators active in the Irish market. As of June 2006, the mobile penetration rate in Ireland was 103 percent, with 4.37 million mobile subscribers.

Broadband use has grown with an increase in the number of licensed operators. Broadband penetration was estimated at 8.8 percent in June 2006, up from 5 percent in 2005. Ireland has adopted EU local loop unbundling (LLU) legislation, and the government has initiated legal action to compel Eircom to complete LLU in order to promote competition and innovation in the DSL market.

Luxembourg

In 2005, Luxembourg began revising administrative procedures to implement the EU Framework Directive to liberalize Member States' telecommunications markets and allow for fairer competition. Despite these efforts, the state-owned P and T company continues to dominate the nation's telecommunications market. In addition, despite a 1998 court ruling opening Luxembourg's small mobile phone market to competition, the wireless communications market remains dominated by only three companies, one of which is half-owned by the state company.

Poland

Telecommunications and Internet investments remain strong in Poland. New competitors (Netia, Orange, Germanos) have entered the cellular market, and well-known Internet presences, such as Google, are locating in Warsaw. Still, the ability of new entrants to compete may have been hindered by the failure of Poland's Electronic Communications Office – UKE – to implement the EU Framework Directive in a timely manner. The UKE continues to battle Polish telecommunications operator TPSA over its monopolistic business practices.

Spain

Access to leased lines in Spain remains problematic because rates do not appear to be based on actual cost. Despite actions by CMT, Spain's NRA, wholesale prices are still above the European average and approximately 100 percent above U.S. prices. This has allowed the incumbent operator Telefónica to offer services to customers at substantially lower rates than competitive carriers.

U.S. companies have complained that Spanish mobile operators are charging excessively high mobile termination rates and that they are squeezed out of the fixed-to-mobile communications market because mobile operators offer their subscribers mobile-to-mobile and fixed-to-mobile calls at below wholesale rates. Spanish anti-trust authorities are considering penalizing these mobile operators.

Evolution of the broadband market has been slow and problematic, and many operators have ceased offering these services. However, Telefónica's market share is being challenged by two operators: Ya.com and Wanadoo. Both of these companies have established partnerships with Spanish fixed and mobile line carriers.

Chapter 9

INVESTMENT BARRIERS

OVERVIEW

The European Commission's mandate on investment issues is evolving. EU Member States negotiate their own bilateral investment protection and taxation treaties and generally retain responsibility for their investment regimes. In many areas, individual Member State policies and practices have a more significant impact on U.S. firms than do EU-level policies and practices.

Under the 1993 Maastricht Treaty, free movement of capital became an EU responsibility and capital controls both among EU Member States and between EU members and third countries were lifted. A few Member States' barriers remain in place, although in particular cases, EU law may supersede these. Right of establishment issues, particularly regarding third countries, are a shared competence between the EU and the Member States. The division of this shared competence varies from sector to sector based on whether the EU has issued regulations in a particular sector. Direct branches of non-EU financial service institutions remain subject to individual Member State authorization and regulation.

The EU requires national treatment for foreign investors in most sectors. EU law, with a few exceptions, requires that any company established under the laws of one Member State must, as a Community undertaking, receive national treatment in all Member States, regardless of its ultimate ownership. However, some restrictions on U.S. investment do exist under EU law and others have been proposed, as discussed below.

OWNERSHIP RESTRICTIONS AND RECIPROCITY PROVISIONS

EU Treaty Articles 43 (establishment) and 56/57 (capital movements) have helped the EU to achieve one of the most hospitable climates for U.S. investment in the world, but some restrictions on foreign direct investment remain in place. Under EU law, the right to provide aviation transport services within the EU is reserved to firms majority-owned and controlled by EU nationals. The right to provide maritime transport services within certain EU Member States is also restricted. EU banking, insurance and investment services directives currently include "reciprocal" national treatment clauses under which a financial services firm from a third country may be denied the right to establish a new business in the EU if the EU determines that the investor's home country denies national treatment to EU service providers. The right of U.S. firms to national treatment in this area was reinforced by the EU's GATS commitments.

After years of discussion, the Council of Ministers finally agreed in March 2004 on a directive on takeover bids ("Takeover Directive"). The original proposal would have banned any national legislation allowing companies to prevent hostile takeovers through the use of defensive measures (e.g., "poison pills" or multiple voting rights). The final directive makes it optional for Member States and companies to maintain a regime that rules out these defensive measures or to opt out of such rules. The European Parliament debated whether to limit the benefits of the new directive to companies that apply the same provisions, (e.g., limiting the right of a board to take defensive measures or to mitigate the role of restrictions on share transfers or voting in a takeover bid). Article 12.3 of the final text is ambiguous as to whether the limitation would apply to non-EU firms, although the preamble of the legislation states that the application of the optional measures is without prejudice to international agreements to which the EC is a party.

The Directive was due to be implemented by the Member States by May 20, 2006. However, only Denmark, France, Hungary, Luxembourg, and the UK met this deadline. Ireland and Germany implemented the Directive after the deadline, and other countries have introduced draft legislation.

Under the 1994 hydrocarbons directive (Directive 94/22/EC), an investor may be denied a license to explore for and exploit hydrocarbon resources if the investor's home country does not permit EU investors to engage in those activities under circumstances "comparable" to those in the EU. These reciprocity provisions thus far have not affected any U.S.-owned firms.

MEMBER STATE PRACTICES

Austria

While European Economic Area (EEA) Member States' banks may operate branches on the basis of their home country licenses, banks from outside the EEA must obtain Austrian licenses to operate in Austria. However, if a non-EEA bank has already obtained a license in another EEA country for the operation of a subsidiary, it does not need a license to establish branch offices in Austria.

Bulgaria

Local companies in which foreign partners have controlling interests must obtain licenses to engage in certain activities, including: production and export of arms/ammunition; banking and insurance; exploration, development, and exploitation of natural resources; and acquisition of property in certain geographic areas. On February 23, 2007, the United States and Bulgaria signed the Treaty on Avoidance of Double Taxation (DTT). The U.S. business community in Bulgaria believes that the DTT will facilitate bilateral investment and trade. The insolvency rules in Bulgaria's Commercial Code and its Law on Public Offering of Securities (2005) have greatly improved the legislative protection for minority shareholders, but enforcement of the law's provisions is inadequate and corporate governance remains weak.

Cyprus

Property Acquisition: Cypriot law imposes significant restrictions on the foreign ownership of real property. Persons not ordinarily resident in Cyprus (whether of EU or non-EU origin) may purchase only a single piece of real estate (not to exceed three donum or roughly one acre) for private use (normally a holiday home). Exceptions can be made for projects requiring larger plots of land (i.e., beyond that necessary for a private residence) but they are difficult to obtain and are rarely granted. The restriction on property acquisition for EU citizens not normally resident in Cyprus will expire in May 2009. (Cyprus received a temporary derogation from the EU *acquis communautaire* on this issue, lasting for five years after accession). The restrictions will continue to apply, however, to non-EU residents, including U.S. nationals.

Tertiary education investment restrictions: Cypriot legislation on foreign investment in tertiary education distinguishes between colleges and universities. Investment in universities, defined as institutions with no fewer than 1,000 students enrolled in a sufficiently diverse range of classes and curricula, is encouraged. Foreign (including non-EU) investors can set up or acquire a university in Cyprus by simply registering a company on the island and following a set of non-discriminatory criteria. By contrast, non-EU investment in colleges is discouraged. Non-EU investors can set up or acquire a local college by registering a company in Cyprus or elsewhere in the EU provided that the company has EU-origin shareholders and directors. As a consequence, non-EU investors are not allowed to participate whether as directors or shareholders in the administration of local colleges.

Investment Restriction in Media Companies: Cyprus also restricts non-EU ownership of local mass media companies to 5 percent or less for individual investors and 25 percent or less for all foreign investors in each individual media company.

Construction: Under the Registration and Control of Contractors Laws of 2001 and 2004, the right to register as a construction contractor in Cyprus is reserved for citizens of EU Member States. Non-EU entities are not allowed to own a majority stake in a local construction company. Non-EU physical persons or legal entities may bid on specific construction projects, but only after obtaining a special license by the Council of Ministers.

Professional Recognition of Real Estate Agents and Other Groups: The current law licensing real estate agents to practice in Cyprus, last amended in 2003, acts as a protectionist measure, creating significant barriers to entry into the profession. Cypriot law recognizes only licensed individuals (not companies) to act as authorized real estate entities and licenses are only granted to individuals who have served as apprentices to licensed individuals for up to eight years. Existing real estate agents have also tried to use the law to restrict the ability of foreign real estate networks to advertise in their own names, although this interpretation of the law is under debate. There are also similar concerns about the transparency of the legislation concerning state recognition and accreditation of several other professions, including medical doctors and civil aviation pilots.

France

There are generally few screening or prior approval requirements for non-EU foreign investment in France. As part of a November 2004 law that streamlined the French Monetary and Financial Code, however, the State Council was directed to define a number of sensitive sectors in which prior approval would be required before acquisition of an equity stake.

A December 2005 government decree lists 11 business sectors in which the French Ministry of Economy, Finance and Industry has the right to monitor and restrict foreign ownership through a system of "prior authorization." These sectors include: businesses involved in the gambling industry, regulated businesses providing private security services, businesses involved in the research and development or manufacture of means of fighting the illegal use of pathogens or toxic substances by terrorists and preventing the adverse health-related consequences of such use, businesses dealing with wiretapping and mail interception equipment, businesses licensed to audit and certify services relating to the security of information technology systems and products, businesses providing goods and services relating to the security of the information systems of public or private-sector companies managing critical infrastructures, and businesses relating to certain dual-use items and technology.

The GOF is working on a draft bill on the protection from foreign takeover bids of 20 French companies defined as "sensitive." In addition, the government implemented the EU anti-takeover directive on March 31, 2006. Implementing legislation allows companies to resort to a U.S. style "poison pill" takeover defense, including granting existing shareholders and employees the right to increase their leverage by buying more shares through stock purchase warrants at a discount in case of an unwanted takeover. The government also asked the state-owned financial institution Caisse de Depots et Consignations (CDC), France's largest institutional investor, to work as a domestic buffer against foreign takeovers by increasing its stakes in French companies. In the name of "economic patriotism," the French government has thus demonstrated an inclination to intervene in potential transnational mergers or to otherwise signal its interest in defending French commercial "champions" from foreign takeover attempts.

Germany

Germany's 2002 takeover law was marginally changed by the implementation of the EU takeover directive. Germany made use of its "opt-out" right and retained measures that allow firms to ward off hostile takeover bids, first at the shareholder level, where management may be given authority at annual shareholder meetings to take necessary measures to guard against unwanted takeover interest; and, second, at the management level, where the managing board may take protective measures upon approval by the supervisory board, bypassing the need for shareholder approval altogether. The EU directive offers companies the choice either to abide by the German law or to "opt-in" to the EU regulation. Companies using the "opt-in" may limit their waiver of Germany's protective measures to companies that also have no measures in place to fend-off hostile takeover bids.

Germany passed legislation in July 2004 requiring notification by foreign entities of investments expected to exceed 25 percent of the equity of German firms engaged in the production of armaments and cryptology technology used for classified government communications. Following an inter-ministerial review, the government may veto such sales within one month of receipt of a notification. The German government expanded the scope of the law in 2005 to include tank and tracked vehicle engines to block a U.S. financial investor from buying a tank engine manufacturer.

Greece

Greek authorities consider local content and export performance when evaluating applications for tax and investment incentives. Such criteria do not appear to be prerequisites for approving investments, however.

Greece has opened its telecommunications market and is in the process of gradually liberalizing its energy sector. At present, however, Greece's inhospitable regulatory framework has hampered efforts by U.S. firms to develop energy production facilities.

U.S. and other non-EU investors receive less advantageous treatment in Greece than domestic or other EU competitors in the banking, mining, maritime, air transport and broadcast industries (which were opened to EU citizens under EU single market rules). For reasons of national security, non-EU investors are restricted in their ability to purchase land in border regions and on certain islands.

Italy

The EU Takeover Directive has not yet been incorporated into Italian law. Current Italian law, which continues to apply pending the enactment in Italy of the EU Directive, requires the target of a takeover or merger bid to obtain authorization from shareholders before undertaking defensive measures to fend off a hostile bid and provides for a break-through rule on the most common pre-bid defensive tactics (i.e., shareholder voting agreements).

With few exceptions, Italy provides national treatment to foreign investors established in Italy or in another EU member state, as required by Article 43 of the EU Treaty. Under current regulations, U.S. and other non-Italian banks must obtain Bank of Italy approval to operate in Italy. Foreign banks face the same capital requirements as banks chartered in Italy. U.S. and other investment firms from non-EU countries may operate with authorization from Italy's securities market regulator, CONSOB. CONSOB may deny authorization to investment firms from countries that discriminate against Italian firms.

Malta

Maltese law requires that anyone buying residential or commercial real estate must obtain a permit from the Minister of Finance. EU citizens and returning Maltese migrants who have lived in Malta for more than five years receive a waiver from these permits. Non-EU citizens are not entitled to this waiver. Despite the restriction, permission to purchase land for commercial or residential purposes is normally granted. No U.S. businesses appear to have been discouraged from investing in Malta because of these restrictions. The restrictions have, however, delayed certain business investment projects involving American businesses.

Romania

A law on securities that was passed in 2004 entitles majority shareholders owning 95 percent of the total stock in a firm to buy residual shares. This law is considered to be a compromise, and provides very limited minority shareholder protection. Some minority shareholders have complained that Romanian authorities do not adequately protect their rights. A continued impediment to foreign investment is Romania's inconsistent legal and regulatory system. Tax laws change frequently and are unevenly enforced. Tort cases often require lengthy, expensive procedures, and judges' rulings are often not enforced.

Chapter 10

ELECTRONIC COMMERCE

U.S. businesses and the U.S. Government continue to monitor potential problems related to data privacy regulation and legal liabilities for companies doing business over the Internet in the EU.

DATA PRIVACY

The EU Data Protection Directive (1995/46) allows the transmission of EU data to third countries only if those countries are deemed by the European Commission to provide an adequate level of protection by reason of its domestic law or of the international commitments it has entered into (Article 25(6)). U.S. companies can only receive or transfer employee and customer information from the EU by using one of the exceptions to the Directive's adequacy requirements or by demonstrating they can provide adequate protection for the transferred data. These requirements can be burdensome for many U.S. industries that rely on data exchange across the Atlantic.

Currently, the Commission has recognized Switzerland, Canada, Argentina, Guernsey, Isle of Man, the U.S. Department of Commerce's Safe Harbor Privacy Principles, and the transfer of Air Passenger Name Record to the U.S. Bureau of Customs and Border Protection as providing adequate protection. The U.S. Safe Harbor framework provides U.S. companies with a simple, streamlined means of complying with the adequacy requirement. The agreement allows U.S. companies that commit to a series of data protection principles (based on the Directive) and that publicly state their commitment by "self-certifying" on a dedicated website (www.export.gov/safeharbor), to continue to receive and transfer personal data from the EU. Signing up to the Safe Harbor is voluntary, but the rules are binding on signatories. A failure to fulfill the commitments of the Safe Harbor framework is actionable either as an unfair and deceptive practice under Section 5 of the FTC Act or, for air carriers and ticket agents, under a concurrent Department of Transportation statute.

The U.S. Government actively supports the Safe Harbor framework and encourages the European Commission and Member States to continue to use the flexibility offered by the Data Protection Directive to avoid unnecessary interruptions in data flows to the United States. Furthermore, the U.S. Government expects the European Commission and EU Member States to fulfill their commitment to inform the U.S. Government if they become aware of any actions that may interrupt data flows to the United States.

BRUSSELS REGULATION

On December 22, 2000, the EU adopted the so-called Brussels Regulation which allows consumers to sue companies in the court of their country of residence, "when the website is directed to [his/her] Member State or to several countries, including that Member State." Industry has complained that the practical effect of this regulation is that companies doing business on the Internet in the EU risk being sued in every EU Member State, as opposed to being subject to the jurisprudence of their country of origin.

Chapter 11

OTHER BARRIERS

HEALTHCARE

Ireland

U.S. healthcare firms have faced difficulties entering Ireland's hybrid public-private health system. To generate sufficient revenues to justify investments in Irish hospitals and equipment, U.S. firms usually seek to treat both private and public patients. The treatment of public patients, however, requires a Service Level Agreement from the Health Service Executive (HSE), the administrative agency that oversees Ireland's hospital system. U.S. firms report difficulties in securing such an agreement from the HSE, despite longstanding problems with the provision of public health services in Ireland.

In the health insurance market, Ireland has espoused "risk equalization," whereby private insurers are required by law to compensate the Voluntary Health Insurance (VHI) Board, a quasi-governmental body, for the additional risk that it accepts in offering community (or equal) rating for policy-holders of different ages and medical profiles. Compensation is to be paid once a certain threshold based on the number of insured is reached, but the Irish government has not clarified the formula for determining the threshold. This ambiguity has been a factor in discouraging U.S. insurance firms from entering the Irish market.

INDEX

A

B

C

D

E

F

G

H

I

N

O

T

U

V

W